I SAILED WITH CHINESE PIRATES

The author on board Lai Choi San's pirate junk

I SAILED WITH CHINESE PIRATES

ALEKO E. LILIUS

HONG KONG
OXFORD UNIVERSITY PRESS
OXFORD   NEW YORK
1991

Oxford University Press

Oxford   New York   Toronto
Petaling Jaya   Singapore   Hong Kong   Tokyo
Delhi   Bombay   Calcutta   Madras   Karachi
Nairobi   Dar es Salaam   Cape Town
Melbourne   Auckland

and associated companies in
Berlin   Ibadan

First published by J. W. Arrowsmith Ltd. 1930
All attempts to trace the copyright holder
have proved unsuccessful

This edition reprinted
in Oxford Paperbacks 1991

ISBN 0 19 585297 4

Printed in Hong Kong by Nordica Printing Co., Ltd.
Published by Oxford University Press, Warwick House, Hong Kong

Dedicated

TO THE MEMORY OF PLUCKY

WENG

ONLY A COOLIE, BUT A
FAITHFUL FRIEND WHO
DIED IN MY SERVICE

PREFACE

I BELIEVE that I have glimpsed a page of the Book of Almost Unbelievable Adventures. Unbelievable, because it has all happened in our time.

And it is still happening.

I expected to find many strange, and perhaps also some gruesome things in Southern China. I found there displayed the naked passions of elemental humanity. And the savageness—and splendour—of it almost stunned me.

I have also met men and women who seemed to be in their natural surroundings only when they were moving in an atmosphere saturated with the nauseating, body-warm smell of blood and the pungent reek of opium. I have heard the clinking of the shiny *fan-tan* " cash " and also of heavy gold coins, real Spanish doubloons from uncovered hoards. I have heard the groaning of tortured prisoners, too.

It is all there to-day, just as it was a millennium ago; and it will be there to-morrow, perhaps until the Day of Judgment, either Divine or human. Gospel or parley will not bring about an immediate change. Only Sword and Fire can do that.

THE AUTHOR.

LIST OF ILLUSTRATIONS

9

FOREWORD

PARTS of this book have been agony to write. It has meant the living over of scenes I prefer to forget. In my search for the unusual, I found more of it than I had bargained for. It may seem strange to the casual reader that one whose profession is journalism should feel reluctant to write his " story " after having gone through adventures such as it is the lot of few men to experience, with the sole object of obtaining " copy." But I can assure them that the agony of re-living such experiences is far greater than that of the actuality that is past.

Had it not been for the insistence of my friend Carl N. Taylor, Professor of English in the University of the Philippines, and a journalist by avocation, the book probably would never have been written. He has collaborated with me to the very limit, and there is hardly a page in the manuscript that has not been the cause of a quarrel between us.

I am also indebted to Mr. Merrill Goddard, Editor of *The American Weekly*, New York ; Miss Marietta Neff, Editor of *Asia*, New York ; Mr. J. Tate, Editor of *Popular Mechanics*, Chicago ; the Editors of the *Sphere*, London ; Captain Victor Pitt-Kethley, Editor of the *Wide World*, London ; and the editors of various Continental European magazines for permission to reprint parts of articles and pictures that have appeared in their publications under my name.

Lastly, I owe a deep debt of gratitude to the American Consular staff at Hong-Kong, who during a very trying phase of my adventures assisted me in every way within their power.

THE AUTHOR.

Zamboanga, P.I.,
   May, 1930.

I SAILED WITH CHINESE PIRATES

PART ONE

THE Hong-Kong Governor-General's secretary, Captain Whyte, had a very frank opinion about journalists, especially journalists interested in the pirates of Bias Bay.

Bias Bay is located only sixty-five miles east of Hong-Kong, and it is inhabited by the most infamous gang of high-sea pirates that infest the South China coast. Why they have been permitted to pursue their "trade" unmolested during modern times is a matter not to be discussed at this point.

I had been assigned by a group of American and European periodicals to gather all possible information regarding these pirates and their activities. The Colonial Secretary very kindly opened his files for my inspection, and after several days of painstaking scrutiny of documents, telegrams, police reports and photographs I emerged from this stack of official blood-and-fire stories with a conviction that the bandits of Bias Bay certainly must know their job. On the other hand, I had got the impression that the pirates of Bias Bay were only tools of somebody higher up—somebody in Canton, Amoy, Swatow, or perhaps even in Hong-Kong.

The pirates undertake their "jobs" after weeks of preparation. During this time they travel back and

forth as passengers aboard the steamers which they have
selected for robbing. Finally, after supplies of arms and
ammunition have been smuggled on board, and the ship
is well out at sea, at a given signal from the leader they
attack the crew. One group storms the bridge, another
attacks the engine-room, and a third keeps the passengers
at bay. The piracy invariably occurs near Bias Bay,
where the ship is brought and the cargo unloaded into
waiting sampans and junks. The rich passengers, both
white and Chinese, are taken ashore to be held for
ransom.

During the last ten years an average of three ships
a year bearing British or foreign flags have been pirated
by this gang. How many Chinese ships and junks they
have attacked is not known.

For almost one hundred years all the ships pirated
on their way to or from Hong-Kong had invariably been
brought to Bias Bay, stripped of everything valuable,
and afterwards released. Until lately the ships' officers
seldom put up an effective resistance, and for a number of
years the sea-rovers did not consider the piracy business
very risky. On the contrary, it was a comparatively safe
and a very remunerative undertaking.

To gain the control of a ship and her officers the
pirates follow a method which can hardly be improved
upon. The bandits, from ten to sixty in number, board
the ships as passengers, some as third class and some—
the leaders and a few trusted men—going as first class
passengers. This arrangement gives them access to all
parts of the ship, with the exception of the bridge, which
is usually protected by grilles and a heavy iron net
reaching all the way around the ship's superstructure.
The entrances through these grilles are guarded by

The captain's bridge protected by a grill

Anti-pirate guard ready for action

S.S. Sui An has been pirated and looted

The third class passengers are kept below behind heavy iron bars
in ships plying between Hong-Kong and Macao

Indian sentries who stand behind steel-armoured plates. These guards are armed with guns and pistols.

The arms of the pirates are, almost without exception, smuggled on board by someone exempt from the minute inspection to which the police subject all other Chinese travellers.

In the case of the piracy of the S.S. *Sunning*, on 15th November, 1926, the excerpts from the official report show clearly the method :—

There seems to be no doubt that the pirates all boarded the vessel at Amoy, and that their weapons were taken aboard for them by some of the stevedores, who, though not on the ship's articles, are invariably allowed to travel on these ships, and have permission to sell goods, *i.e.* fruit, cigarettes, cakes, tea, and act as hawkers to the passengers. These men have every opportunity for smuggling.

With the ship under way, the arms distributed, the leaders stationed at strategic points all over the ship, the pirates await the opening of one of the doors in the grilles or the change of the guards ; then there is a shrill whistle, or a shot, or perhaps a hellish beating of the gongs. It is the signal for the attack.

During their years of more or less undisturbed buccaneering the pirates have developed an intelligence service which supplies them with correct information regarding ships' locations and their cargoes—whether they are carrying gold, silver specie, bar silver, or other valuable cargo, such as opium or silk. Whenever there has been a piracy, and the loot has amounted to, say, $60,000 to $100,000, the individual pirates who have been caught have not possessed much loot beyond a few articles taken from the passengers, and in rare

B

cases a few hundred dollars in money. Invariably the stolen property is delivered to the leaders, who see that it promptly disappears inland, where it can never be accounted for; the ships are then permitted to return to Hong-Kong, or to continue on their voyages.

Many facts seem to bear out the existence of an intrenched central organization. It appears, however, that on one occasion the pirates of Bias Bay decided to do business on their own account, and a very curious thing happened. Had it not been for the fact that one man was murdered and another wounded, the affair would have been an appropriate comic opera subject.

On 3rd October, 1924, the steamer *Ning Shin* was pirated, and, as usual, brought to Bias Bay, where the cargo, consisting of thirty cases of silver bars, value 97,000 taels (the par value of a tael is about 34 cents U.S. currency [1930]), was brought ashore and divided among the pirates. Very much to the Hong-Kong authorities' surprise, the Canton officials immediately responded to the usual request from Hong-Kong to round up the bandits. They dispatched troops to the Bias Bay area. The commander of this expedition against the village of Nim Shan, the home village of pirates, was a certain Yung Fai Ting. The raid resulted in the rounding up of all the pirates and the recovery of most of the silver, but the pirates were released on payment of a large sum, and all the silver was appropriated by Yung Fai Ting, who apparently acted on orders from the central body. One of the pirates was ultimately caught by the British police, and he admitted that their leader had been a certain Lam Tsoi Sau. He said the pirates had gone to Hong-Kong, where they had stayed on the Hung Ong boarding-house before leaving for Shanghai, where they purchased the arms used in the raid. He further testified that he had received forty pieces (bars) of silver, forty dollars in one-dollar coins, and some serge. The number of pirates had been eighteen ; they had come from different villages near Bias Bay. He deeply lamented the interference of the " greedy " Chinese commander.

Hong-Kong was, as a matter of fact, a sea-rovers' nest before the advent of the British, and so was Macao. And both cities have had large numbers of pirates among the Chinese population ever since. There is probably no official record for the whole of the last fifty years of how many and what ships have been pirated and brought to Bias Bay, but there is a list of piracies during the last, say, twenty or thirty years. It is by no means complete, as it has been well-nigh impossible to ascertain the number of Chinese ships that have been attacked and looted, but the record of the British and other foreign ships is fairly complete. This list makes rather interesting reading, and proves that the piracy question cannot be a matter of slight concern.

Following is the list, since 1921, of the ships and the dates when pirated, also the losses in money, jewellery, property of the ship or the passengers. The reader's attention is drawn to the losses in lives and wounded :—

Year.	Date.	Name of Vessel.	Losses in dollars. (Hong-Kong currency.)
1921.	Jan. 22.	Steam launch *Kung Hong* .	22,000
	Dec. 15.	S.S. *Kwong Lee* . .	120,000
	Dec. 18.	Steam launch *Wah Sun* .	21,000
1922.	May 22.	Steam launch *Wa Sun* .	5,000

Year.	Date.	Name of Vessel.	Losses in dollars. (Hong-Kong currency.)
1922.	Oct. 4.	Steam launch *San On* . (Weapons were brought on board in a clock.)	Total amount not given, but the passengers lost all their jewellery, money and clothing.
	Nov. 19.	S.S. *Sui An* . . . (The captain and a passenger wounded. Two Indian guards killed.)	34,000
1923.	Oct. 23.	S.S. *Sunning* . . .	20,000
	Dec. 27.	S.S. *Hydrangea* . .	23,389 10,000 } in cargo.
1924.	Oct. 3.	S.S. *Ning Shin* . .	(97,000 taels in bullion.)
1925.	Jan. 13.	S.S. *Hong Wha* . . (The pirates thought that the ship carried bullion, and came as passengers from Singapore.)	53,360
	Dec. 18.	S.S. *Tung Chow* . .	30,000 (bullion). 10,000 (other ———— values). 40,000
1926.	Feb. 5.	S.S. *Jade*	82,000 (bullion).
	Mar. 6.	S.S. *Tai Yau* . . .	Unknown.
	Mar. 25.	S.S. *Hsin Kong* . .	Unknown.
	July 13.	S.S. *Kwang Lee* . .	Unknown.
	Aug. 21.	S.S. *Sandviken* . . (Norwegian registry.)	Unknown.
	Oct. 1.	S.S. *Hsin Fung* . .	Unknown.
	Nov. 15.	S.S. *Sunning* . . . Killed : one European passenger, one Annamite passenger and four pirates (three shot, one drowned). Wounded : Chief Engineer, five Chinese and three pirates (later executed in Hong - Kong). Missing : four Chinese from the compradore's staff. Seven pirates in a drifting boat apparently drowned.	The whole ship burned and severely damaged.
	Dec. 22.	S.S. *Heng An* . . .	Unknown.
1927.	Jan. 2.	S.S. *Yuan An* . . .	Unknown.
	Jan. 27.	S.S. *Seang Bee* . .	Unknown.

Year.	Date.	Name of Vessel.	Losses in dollars. (Hong-Kong currency.)
1927.	Mar. 22.	S.S. *Hop Sang* . . (It was after this piracy that the British finally lost their patience and raided the Bias Bay villages, independently of the Chinese authorities.)	Unknown.
	May 6.	S.S. *Feng Pu* . . .	10,000
	July 19.	S.S. *Solviken* . . . (Norwegian registry.) The Captain murdered in his cabin ; eight Chinese kidnapped.	20,400 (In gold bars.) 22,900 (cargo stolen.)
	Oct. 21.	S.S. *Irene* . . . Killed: one Chinese steward. (This piracy was intercepted by the British Submarine L4, commanded by Lieut. Halahan, recently knighted for this deed. The submarine tried to stop the ship, but was finally forced to send a shot through her hull, setting the vessel on fire. However, he rescued the ship and her 238 passengers. Many of the pirates were brought to justice, but several of them were drowned jumping overboard when the submarine approached the pirated ship.)	—
1928.	Sept. 29.	S.S. *Anking* . . . Killed : The Chief Engineer and one Chinese quartermaster. Wounded : The Master of the ship.	80,000
	Dec. 12.	S.S. *Wong She Kung* .	5,000
1929.	Sept. 20.	S.S. *Delhi Maru* . . (Several of the Indian guards shot.) This is the first ship of Japanese registry that has ever been pirated in South China.	As yet unknown.

Year.	Date.		Name of Vessel.	Losses in dollars. (Hong-Kong currency.)
1929.	Dec.	8.	S.S. *Haiching* . . . Killed : Third Officer F. F. Woodward, one Indian guard, seven male and two female Chinese. The killed pirates are at the moment of this writing not accoun- ted for, but are supposed to have been at least ten. Several children drowned. Wounded : Chief Officer Robert Perry, one quarter- master, one guard and twenty Chinese, including the members of the crew.	The ship burned and badly damaged. Most passengers lost all their property.

The piracies on the West River and along the coast above Bias Bay all the way up to Shanghai are not accounted for in the above list, although most of them could undoubtedly be traced as instigated by the same common source.

Of all the piracies that of the S.S. *Sunning* was probably the most spectacular and interesting, because the officers not only fought against overwhelming odds but actually *recaptured* the ship, although with heavy losses in dead and wounded.

Let us take a look at the files of the confidential reports on this case lodged in the Colonial Secretary's office :—

Piracy of S.S. *Sunning*, 15th November, 1926. Butterfield and Swire, Agents.

Left Shanghai with one hundred Chinese and two European passengers and general cargo on Friday, 12th November, for Hong-Kong via Coast Ports. Six European officers and a native crew. Her first port was Amoy. Left Amoy Monday, 15th November, at 9.30 a.m., and when near Chilang Point (south of Amoy) at about 4 p.m. a sudden attack was made by approximately twenty-five pirates, who had embarked as passengers. They overpowered the guard at the grille—giving access to the upper deck, the bridge and the engine-room—just as the guard were changing duty, and rushed the bridge, taking all officers unawares. The two guards not on duty were imprisoned in their cabins.

Having gained possession of the ship and relieved every one of their weapons, the pirates ordered the captain to steer to Chilang Point and proceeded to loot the ship.

The pirates expected to find ten cases of specie, worth about $500,000, but these had not been shipped. The "Number One Pirate" told the captain that it had cost them $3,000 to get aboard the ship. They now started to loot the compradore's safe and the belongings of the passengers.

The officers on the bridge as well as the engine-room staff were covered by the pirates' guns. Mr. Lapsley (later killed), of the Eastern Extension Telegraph Co., acted as an interpreter. The only woman passenger was a Russian lady.

The pirates remained in control of the ship until 1 a.m., when two of the ship's officers, the second engineer, William Orr, and the third engineer, Andrew Duncan, who had secretly collected a few weapons which had been overlooked in their cabins by the pirates while searching them, felled two of their guards on the bridge and recaptured it, shooting at a third pirate, who came up to the rescue of his comrades and who thereupon hastily retreated. The officers now took possession of the arms of the felled pirates, and with these weapons covered the approaches to the bridge. They also got up the European passengers from below through a hatch skylight in the deck.

The pirates now advanced from the stern of the ship in two parties, using the chief engineer, George Cormack, whom they had brought up from below as a shield by pushing him ahead of them on one side and members of the crew, chiefly cabin boys, for the same purpose on the other side.

The Chief Engineer and the cabin boys were wounded in the arms, thigh and chest by bullets from the bridge.

The scheme failed and the pirates retreated.

The pirates now decided to set fire to the ship amidships, so as to smoke out the people on the bridge. The fire was started under the bridge at 3 a.m.

The officers now managed to turn the ship, placing it broadside to the wind, thus diverting the flames and smoke from the bridge and *actually smoking out the pirates*, who had entrenched themselves in the poop.

Then the pirates had to abandon the ship. They went in two boats, possibly taking Mr. Lapsley with them, as he has not been seen or heard from since the officers regained the control of the bridge.

One hour later, when the fire had assumed very much larger dimensions, the rest of the armed pirates, ten altogether, left in a second dinghy.

The ship's officers were now able to turn their attention to checking the fire. They also succeeded in lowering one of the ship's remaining lifeboats, which was actually burning at the time. While being manned it drifted off from the ship, owing to the ropes of the lowering tackle burning away, and after a hazardous journey of nine hours was picked up at sea by a Norwegian steamer. This boat had been manned by the second officer, third engineer, the wireless operator, a quartermaster and the Russian lady passenger.

The news of the piracy reached Hong-Kong, and several warships were immediately dispatched to the scene of the outrage. H.M.S. *Bluebell* was the first to reach the spot. She sighted the boat with the fleeing pirates and picked them up. One man jumped overboard and was drowned. When the *Bluebell* closed on the boat arms were seen to be thrown overboard. The occupants were turned over to the police later.

At 5 a.m. the burning *Sunning* had been sighted by two merchantmen. The S.S. *Ka Ying* lowered a boat and made for the *Sunning*, who requested an armed party to be put on board, and later reported that they had thirteen suspects under arrest. Several pirates perished in the smoke and fire they had themselves originated.

It is only fair to state that the plucky officers and crew were later rewarded by the Hong-Kong Government with sums varying from £25 to £100 each.

From the first the Bias Bay crowd has had, and continues to have, the laugh on law and order, whether represented by British or Chinese authorities. While this state of affairs exists there is no hope that these outrageous piracies will be discontinued.

*   *   *   *   *

Having discovered so much, my next step seemed to be to go to Bias Bay. Everybody, from the Consul-General to the room-boy in my hotel, told me that I was mad even to think of such a thing. It is simply not done.

Therefore, when I approached the good Captain Whyte, he plainly told me that I and all other journalists were nuisances, and I received the impression that it is not *comme il faut* to speak of pirates and piracies to any high official in Hong-Kong. I had hoped that the Captain would arrange for me to go with one of the customs or police boats that occasionally travel in those districts, but I was told that this would be out of the question.

But to Bias Bay I was determined to go.

I crossed over to Typhoon Bay in Kowloon, and went from junk to junk trying to persuade their captains to take me as a passenger to Bias Bay, but they all declined. Finally, one of them admitted that I had been expected, and that the harbour-master had forbidden the boat owners to have anything to do with me.

Still, there was one way out. My purse did not permit me to buy a junk or a motor-launch, but one could always go to Macao and there hire a junk to take one anywhere one wished to go.

So one morning I boarded the steamer *Sui An*, a much-pirated coast steamer, equipped with steel grilles, heavy armour-plate along the bulwarks, and iron nets enclosing the bridge. Clumsily the steamer turned in mid-stream, steamed out under the Gibraltar-like heights of the Peak, passed the sleepy sampans sailing with the tide down the straits between Kowloon and Victoria, and finally reached the open bay.

Not so many years ago the pirates launched an attack on the *Sui An*, killing and wounding a few of her officers and several of the crew, and robbing the passengers of their jewellery and money. As usual the pirates had disguised themselves as passengers. To-day the *Sui An* is fully prepared to repulse any new attempts by the pirates to take possession of her. The third class passengers are kept below deck, behind heavy iron bars ; and the bridge, the entrance to the engine-room, and the skylights amidships are protected with cage-like grilles. The ship also carries heavily armed Sikh guards, who are supposed to protect the passengers against the buccaneers.

On this morning a Portuguese and I were the only passengers on board. He was a sea captain, born and reared in Macao. Naturally, he knew all the ins and outs of the charming little Portuguese Colony. I ventured to ask him what he knew about pirates.

" Oh, plenty ! "

"Now, what do you mean by plenty?" I urged
him on.

"Oh, I know them all."

I had come 10,000 miles to obtain, or try to obtain,
an idea of pirates and piracies, had gone through stacks
of official documents, mingled with secretaries and their
secretaries and their secretaries, spent weeks trying to
discover clues, only to come across a shabby Portuguese
who casually informed me that he knew all about pirates
and piracies in these waters.

He did not look like a braggart, and he told me that
as a child he had played with the children of pirates,
and that the "trade" of buccaneering was quite a
natural means of livelihood among a certain class of
the seafaring gentry plying the waters between West
River and Macao.

Buccaneering among these people is an inherited
trade. The pirate chiefs of to-day have inherited their
junks and property from their fathers and forefathers,
and many of the pirates have built forts on the small
islands in the West River Delta, and have organized
veritable war-fleets for the purpose of levying taxes on
the cargo junks passing their territories.

Did nobody disturb them? I asked. What about the
authorities, both Portuguese and Chinese? What about
the British?

He laughed.

"The Chinese are too busy with their own wars, and
the Portuguese and the British have nothing to say on
matters concerning territories outside their respective
jurisdictions."

"I'd like to meet some pirates," I said. "Would it
be possible for you to introduce me?"

He assured me that it would be the simplest matter in the world. He would simply call on a man he knew, the captain of a junk which sailed up and down the coast. My Portuguese friend was certain that the man was in Macao, and that I would have a chance to speak to him. We made an appointment for a meeting the same afternoon in a gambling-house.

*   *   *   *   *

The Sun Tai gambling-house, a three-storied *fan-tan* den, was the largest " casino " in the colony. Half-naked people stood around a long table and staked their money on the number of coins that would be left when the man at the end of the table had finished raking in the heaped-up " cash " with his chopsticks, four pieces at a time. There can be only one, two, three, or four chips left over. If there are only two left, then those who have bet their money on " 2 " receive three times their stake, minus 10 per cent. to the house, while all the others are the losers.

I sat for a couple of hours upon the second-floor balcony observing how people lost and made money. Then I placed a few bets myself, for who could resist this novel form of gambling ? Novel for me, at least, although in reality it is probably like everything else in China, thousands of years old. So long as I bet at random, now on " 4," now on " 1," then on " 4 " again, and then on " 3," luck seemed to be with me ; but as soon as I thought I had mastered the game I lost. Betting again at random, I not only regained my losses, but laid up a sizable pile besides. As I was cashing in on a rather heavy bet somebody touched my shoulder. Turning, I saw an undersized Chinese standing before me and smiling sagely. I noticed that he had abnormally small hands, with yellow-stained fingers, that his head was clean-shaven, and that he was dressed in a long, blue silk gown, felt slippers, and a soiled sun-helmet.

" Stop gambling when luck smilee. Lose money, makee heavy heart."

I hated to be interrupted, even by a well-meaning philosopher. But he continued : " Poltuguese man, gleat fliend, sent this Chinaman talkie talkie tlip top-side Hong-Kong."

I was not very well versed in the intricacies of pidgin-English, but I knew enough to understand that my Portuguese friend, who apparently was also a friend of " this Chinaman," had sent him to discuss with me the possibilities of a trip to a place beyond Hong-Kong. So far so good. I nodded as though I understood everything he was trying to tell me.

The man smiled ingratiatingly.

" Come. Go see talkie this Chinaman's house."

So we went to " this Chinaman's " house. We rode in rickshaws through the crooked, narrow streets lined with ancient Latin houses painted yellow, green, rose, and light blue ; past a Mexican style plaza paved in wavy mosaic patterns and surrounded with palm trees ; turned into a lane, and finally stopped in front of a low wrought-iron gate through which " this Chinaman " led me into his home. It was a European house, with nothing Chinese about it, but it nestled within a lovely garden as Oriental as the house was foreign. A man-servant, whose face was the meanest I had ever seen, and made even more horrible by a single knife scar reaching from the corners of his mouth to the lobes of his ears, brought us the conventional tea ; and the side glances with which he favoured me while serving us made me shiver. Truly this man was a type Stevenson would have loved to characterize. He looked a pirate all right. I put him down as the chief cut-throat, or someone of no less importance. But I felt more comfortable when my friend the Portuguese captain appeared and the pow-wow began.

I was not a policeman? Nor a Government agent? Why did I wish to go to Bias Bay, anyway? These and a thousand other things the Chinese wanted to know.

I tried to explain as diplomatically and convincingly as I could that only foolish journalistic curiosity impelled me to go there, and that I made my living by writing. Fortunately, I had brought my last book with me, an account of my adventures in the Chinese Civil War of 1927, which had just been published abroad. The book was full of pictures of generals, marching troops, battles, and messy executions. My host became deeply interested in the pictures of the beheadings, and sat looking at them for a long time, probably philosophically visualizing the ultimate end of his own career.

Did I expect to write a book like this about my trip with him? Full of pictures? And would I give him and his family a few copies?

I most certainly would!

Hm—m! Well, he had an uncle in Bias Bay, he bragged. He could probably take me there for, say, fifty dollars Hong-Kong money.

When would he be ready to sail? He hesitated. I should come back in a week's time.

I returned to Hong-Kong feeling that I was on the right track. However, as I had a whole week on my hands I decided to do a bit more investigating, but where to begin I had no idea. The police did not want to help me. And one does not go along the streets of

Hong-Kong asking every Chinese one meets: "Say, old chap, are you a pirate? If so, please tell me all about it." But luck was with me.

Walking one day along the steep, hilly streets, and looking into curio shop windows, I noticed a man leaning against a casement. His right ear was missing. Where it should have been there was a great black hole in her skull. Putting aside all thought of manners, I pointed, tourist-like, at the place where his ear should have been, and asked him what had happened to it. He smiled broadly.

"Chinee pilates choppee off ear. Send him by my blother. He! He! He!"

"You don't say! Tell me all about it!"

I stepped into his store and sat down. A boy brought tea, and when we had tasted it the earless individual suggested that I should buy some jade rings. I told him I was interested. I was figuring how I could get the man to talk, so I bought a little trinket, and told him that I was coming back very soon to buy more. The man became so enthusiastic that I thought he was going to take down the whole shop. Apparently business had not been brisk.

"By the way," I said casually, as I was about to leave, "tell me how you lost your ear."

He turned and opened a drawer in a carved teak-wood chest, took out a small package done up in dirty silk, and unrolled it, disclosing a dried and blackened human ear—his own. But he would not tell me much about his adventure. He had been kidnapped by the Bias Bay crowd. While a prisoner among them he had been treated fairly well, but all his letters to his relatives begging for ransom had been ignored. Then the pirates had debated for some time whether they should cut off one of his fingers, the tip of his nose, or an ear, finally deciding to let him settle the question; so he had suggested that they cut off his ear. Forthwith this memento had been dispatched with a letter, warning his family that if their dear relative was not ransomed "plenty quick" his head would be coming next. And they had ransomed him!

*   *   *   *   *

The day before I was to return to Macao to keep my appointment with "this Chinaman," there was a knock at my door in the Peninsula Hotel. A Chinese, dressed in European clothes, opened the door and walked in. He did not give me his name, and he came straight to the point.

"I am sorry to bother you," he said in excellent English, "but I have heard that you wish to go to Bias Bay."

The thought flashed through my mind that he had probably come to offer his assistance in the venture, but I was disappointed when he continued:

"I have come to tell you not to go. They think you are from the Secret Service. You will have a very hard time if you go."

I decided to convince him that I was not a policeman. I showed him newspaper clippings of some of my articles.

"Policemen do not run around the world and tell everybody about what they see and learn. All I want is to go to Bias Bay, take a look at the town, shake hands —if possible—with a few murderers, and get out alive. I'd like also to take a few photographs to illustrate my story, but if that is impossible I am content to leave the camera at home."

One of the twelve gambling-houses of Macao

The croupier in a Macao fan-tan den

"We rode in rickshaws through the crooked, narrow streets"
(p. 29)

The " Line " of Hong-Kong where Madame Pompadour's
house was situated

I was certain that the fellow was some kind of emissary, or spy, or perhaps an agent, of the Hong-Kong Government. Quite bluntly I asked :

" Now, who are you, and how the devil do you know that I want to go to Bias Bay ? "

Whereupon he smiled and bowed himself out of my room.

*   *   *   *   *

The next day I went back to Macao. There I saw " this Chinaman," who was full of smiles and excuses ; he told me to come back in a few days. He was not yet ready to go. Unexpected delays had occurred.

So I returned to Hong-Kong.

On the morning after my arrival I went to the jade shop. There was the Earless One leaning against the door-facing as usual, smiling invitingly.

" Come back, buy more jade, master ? "

" Yes, let me see what you have to-day."

He showed me a few things, and again I bought a trinket.

This time he told me that one of his friends had had better luck than he while being kept a hostage in Bias Bay ; his ransom had been paid promptly ; consequently he had retained both his ears.

Could I see this man ? What was his name.

The Earless One gave me the name—Chang Liu— and said he thought the meeting could be arranged. When ? Oh, by and by.

*   *   *   *   *

Once more I went to Macao. And once more " this Chinaman " offered excuses and said that he would surely sail soon, but that he had spoken to Number One Master,

c

and he did not think he could carry me for less than $100.00 Mex. a day. The actual trip to Bias Bay would require perhaps three days; we should remain there one day, and spend two more days on the return to Hong-Kong. That would mean an expenditure of $600. I hesitated. Then I asked him if he was certain that the price would not be raised the next time I came. He assured me in a hurt tone that such would not be the case.

There seemed to be nothing left for me to do except to return to Hong-Kong yet another time. Somewhat disgruntled, I caught the next boat. I was beginning to doubt the possibility of ever getting to Bias Bay.

This time the Earless One promised to introduce me to Chang Liu. We were going to meet him in a Chinese restaurant at West Point where we would have dinner together. West Point is the purely Chinese part of Hong-Kong. It is filled with " sing-sing " houses, opium dens, low-class brothels, and an occasional luxurious restaurant decorated with gilt dragons, silk paintings and costly embroidered draperies. It was in one of these restaurants that Chang Liu awaited us. Although I was going to be the host, he had already ordered the food; and a delicious dinner it was. He made it clear to me from the beginning that he was going to " foot the bill," and that, as he had *heard* about me, he was going to show me the town.

He was a personable chap, about thirty years of age, well-dressed, and—what was more important to me— he spoke perfect English. He was undoubtedly well educated, and he told me that he had travelled in the United States and England. But in manners and appearance he was thoroughly Chinese. He was affable enough and a pleasant talker upon every subject except piracy. That was one thing he positively refused to talk about. At last I decided that I was pushing the subject too rapidly, and feigned to lose interest in piracy.

When the meal was ended and the last tones of the sing-song girl's squeaky voice had died away, and she had been sent out, I suggested that we make a party of the rest of the evening, and that I be the host. It was my intention to show Chang Liu such a pleasant evening that he would think it worth while to cultivate my acquaintance; consequently we proceeded to "paint" the town, and we "painted" it thoroughly.

About midnight we rambled into a dive kept by a European woman whom I shall call Madame Pompadour, because her name was nothing like that, and although she is a thorough sinner, I must admit that she treated me fairly. I have no desire to cause her inconvenient questioning by the authorities.

She recognized Chang Liu at once.

"Hello, Chang, you old pirate," she greeted him, "who's your friend?"

Those words, "you old pirate," made me prick up my ears.

There was another lady in the house, and beautiful indeed she was. La Belle Marie will fit her as well as any other name. Chang Liu melted before her glances like butter in the sun, and I was left alone with Madame.

"You know, I used to be beautiful," she said, "but I have lost my teeth now. Come again next week when I get my new ones. But where did you meet this pirate?"

"What do you mean by 'pirate'? If I were you, I should not talk about it. I probably know Chang Liu better than you do. Maybe I am a pirate myself. By the way," I lied, "we are going out of town soon."

I threw out the bait and she became interested.

" When ? "

" Never mind ! You just sit and watch."

" You'd better be careful."

" Careful about what ? "

She looked at me in astonishment. " Are you trying to pull my leg, or are you trying to make me talk ? "

" Look here, Madame Pompadour, or whatever your name is, I believe you should know who and what I am."

" Don't talk too much if you don't want to."

" I am here to write up the pirates . . ."

" Oh, is that so ? Well, you won't find out anything from me. I don't know anything. Besides, if Chang Liu wishes to tell you, it is up to him. You know, I was very beautiful once, but now my teeth are gone, but I will be all right next week when I get the new ones."

" Look here," I said to the Earless One the next day, " you told me that Chang Liu had been kidnapped like you and held for ransom. You are an infernal liar ! He is a pirate himself—and more power to him."

Then I pushed the Earless One into his shop and banged the door behind us. He finally admitted that Chang Liu was a pirate, and that he had asked the Earless One to invite me to dinner in order that he might find out all about me. Then to my surprise the Earless One told me that Chang Liu had liked me.

Shortly after noon, two days later, I received a telephone call.

" This is me . . . "

I recognized the toothless voice of Madame Pompadour.

" Come over at once. Your pirate is here."

I flew. I could not get to her house soon enough.

But I met with bad luck. I was received in the doorway
by La Belle Marie and another silly, ravishingly beautiful
little thing. They called loudly for champagne, and
executing a war-dance, got me into a side-room. I asked
after Madame Pompadour, but was informed that she
was "busy." That evening cost me the price of two
bottles of champagne. At last Madame sailed in.

"Your pirate was here," she chirped, "but he beat it
as soon as he found out that I had called you. He paid
these two girls well to keep you away until he had made
his exit."

*   *   *   *   *

I was thoroughly disgusted with all pirates, both those
of Hong-Kong and those of Macao.

I had engaged Moon, a young Chinese, as an
interpreter, house-boy, and cook, and together we went
to Macao to have a last chat with "this Chinaman," and
to tell him exactly what I thought of him and all Chinese
pirates.

"This Chinaman" greeted me with a smile.

"Velly good you come to-day. Number One Master
she here."

Then I noticed the presence of a Chinese woman in
the room. I bowed. Hardly acknowledging my greeting,
she began a severe cross-examination with Moon trans-
lating her rapid questions. Judging from her questions,
she was the Number One Master "this Chinaman" had
spoken of, and he himself was only a subordinate. She
mentioned casually that she had been away on " business "
and regretted if I had been delayed thereby. Her
captain, she assured me, making a graceful gesture with
one of her small, well-shaped hands towards "this
Chinaman," could not do anything without her permission.

She was going to sail the next morning at five. I could go along. The price would be forty-three dollars a day. Why just forty-three I never had a chance to ask. All previous figures, therefore, were automatically invalidated.

It happened that she was going in the direction of Bias Bay, she said, and she was willing to take me there and bring me back. But there would be some delay, for she had business to transact on the way—very serious business. The delay, however, would be insignificant, she explained. Then as an afterthought, did I know that the trip would be rather dangerous?

"Dangerous? Why?"

She smiled, but did not answer.

*   *   *   *   *

Here was I, an American journalist, getting the chance of a lifetime, to sail with Chinese pirates to the central nest of the most merciless gang of high-seas robbers in the world, in an armoured junk commanded by a female pirate. Small wonder that I could hardly believe in my luck.

What a woman she was! Rather slender and short, her hair jet black, with jade pins gleaming in the knot at the neck, her ear-rings and bracelets of the same precious apple-green stone. She was exquisitely dressed in a white satin robe fastened with green jade buttons, and green silk slippers. She wore a few plain gold rings on her left hand; her right hand was unadorned. Her face and dark eyes were intelligent—not too Chinese, although purely Mongolian, of course—and rather hard. She was probably not yet forty.

Every move she made and every word she spoke told plainly that she expected to be obeyed, and as I had occasion to learn later, she *was* obeyed.

Our ship was hidden among the junks of Macao

" We glided out into mid-stream " (*p*. 42)

Lai Choi San

She was now to be obeyed, and obeyed she was

What a character she must be! What a wealth of material for a novelist or journalist! Merely to write her biography would be to produce a tale of adventure such as few people dream of.

That evening I heard from an American who had sailed the waters around Macao for fifteen years the following story about this remarkable woman :—

"Her name is Lai Choi San. So many stories centre about her that it is almost impossible to tell where truth ends and legend begins. As a matter of fact, she might be described as a female Chinese version of Robin Hood. They have much in common. Undoubtedly she is the Queen of the Macao pirates. I have never seen her. I have almost doubted her existence until you told me of meeting her. She is said to have inherited the business and the ships from her father, after the old man had gone to his ancestors 'with his slippers on' during a glorious fight between his men and a rival gang. The authorities had given him some sort of refuge here in Macao, with the secret understanding that he and his gang should protect the colony's enormous fishing fleets and do general police duty on the high seas. He even obtained the title of *Inspector* from somebody in authority, and that, of course, placed him morally far above the other pirate gangs.

"He owned seven fully-armoured junks when he died. To-day Lai Choi San owns twelve junks ; nobody seems to know how or when she acquired the additional five, but it is certain that she has them. She has barrels of money, and her will is law.

"You may ask," he continued, "why I call them pirates, since their job is only to 'guard' the numerous fishing craft. However, the other gangs want the same

privileges as the present 'inspectors' have, therefore
they harass and plunder any ship or village they can
lay their hands upon.   They kidnap men, women and
children, hold them for ransom, ransack their homes,
and burn their junks and sampans.   It is up to the
protectors to undo the work of these others and to
avenge any wrong done them.   Naturally, there is bitter
and continuous warfare between these gangs.

"This avenging business is where the piratical
characteristics of the 'protectors' come in.   There is
frequent and profitable avenging going on wherever the
various gangs meet.   Lai Choi San is supposed to be the
worst of them all ; she is said to be both ruthless and
cruel.   When her ships are merely doing patrol duty she
does not bother to accompany them, but when she goes
out 'on business' she attends to it personally.   When
she climbs aboard any of her ships there is an ill-wind
blowing for someone."

*   *   *   *   *

An orange-coloured haze hung over the hills of
Lappa.   Slowly the brown sails of our ship crept up,
while the barefooted crew scurried back and forth upon
the decks.   Finally the junk was clear to heave away.

On a nearby junk a Taoist priest in demon-red robes
kowtowed and burned fire crackers to his special deity
in order to drive away the evil spirits—all this for a few
cents silver.

I was dazed !   It was difficult to believe in my luck.
At last I was actually tramping the deck of an honest-
to-goodness pirate ship !

Our junk lay hidden among many other similar
craft.   It would have been impossible to pick it out from

the shore, and I wondered how the captain would manœuvre us out from such a crowded jumble of boats. But I did not remain in ignorance long. Members of the crew lowered a dinghy, rowed out some distance, and dropped an anchor. Then the dinghy returned, and all hands hauled upon the anchor line until the junk began to move slowly forward. Then the manœuvre was repeated until we had worked ourselves out into the open water. Hardly a sound was to be heard on board—only the shuffling feet of the crew.

I took a look at the crew. Here in South China I had been used to small, narrow-chested, almost effeminate men; but these fellows were almost giants—muscular, heavy - chested, half - naked, hard - looking—real bandit types. Some of them wore the wide-brimmed hat such as one sees all over Southern China. Some had tied red kerchiefs around their heads and necks.

There was nothing for me to do but climb up on the poop and make myself as inconspicuous as possible. I felt in the mood to do just that too—a white man, an intruder, searching for unusual " copy." What right, after all, had I to pry into their secrets ? I was not a Secret Service man, nor a Government employee, whose business it was to find out all about these pirate clans ; yet that was slight assurance that I should return unharmed.

My boy, Moon, did not venture any comments. I believe he was fully as dazed as his master. Still, he was loyal enough to hang on at the rate of $1.00 Mex. per day. No European servant would have done it.

There were twelve smooth-bore, medieval-looking cannons on board, and two rather modern ones. Along the bulwarks of the junk were bolted rows of heavy iron plates. The ammunition, both powder and shot, was kept amidships, the heavier shot being stored in a magazine just abaft the foremast. Rifles and pistols were kept in a separate cabin on the poop, next to the captain's quarters.

*   *   *   *   *

We glided out into midstream.

The rays of the sun had begun to penetrate the haze, and a slight breeze filled the sails. In a few minutes we were outside Macao Harbour, and the heavy camouflaging plates were lifted away from the sides of the ship and placed along the deck. The crew pushed the guns forward, and we became a pirate ship, with rows of ugly, grinning cannons along her sides and a crew which—so help me, gods !—I should not have liked to command.

We hailed a boat, or rather a boat hailed us. The junk hove to and we came almost to a standstill ; then the boat approached us and three women boarded the ship.

One of them I recognized as Lai Choi San. But what a different Lai Choi San ! Yesterday I had seen her in a white satin robe, with green jade ornaments ; to-day she was entirely transformed. Now she wore a jacket-like blouse and black trousers made of the strong, glossy material commonly used by coolies for garments. Her two *amahs* were dressed in similar fashion.

As soon as she stepped on board she kicked off her slippers, and for the rest of the voyage padded about bare-footed. No greetings were exchanged. After a few curt words to the captain, Lai Choi San, with a gesture of her hand, dismissed the boat which had brought her to the ship, and the junk swung out into the wind.

Lai Choi San and her two amahs

They don't look fierce, but they are

" She had singled out a large black junk with three yellow sails "
(p. 45)

Ready for action

Lai Choi San went straight up to her cabin on the poop. This cabin was about as large as an ordinary grand piano box. One could not have stood upright in it ; even when squatting there was scarcely head-room. However, the interior was lavishly decorated with intricate hardwood carvings, embellished here and there with dashes of bright colour. A tiny image of the Goddess A-Ma, the patroness of all seafaring people, hung against the wall next to a small ancestral tablet bearing the name of Lai Choi San's father.

Through the open door I saw her take an incense stick, light it, and thrust it into a pewter vase in front of the tablet. Then she emerged, her two *amahs* following her.

As a matter of fact, those two *amahs* never left her presence.

Lai Choi San's favourite observation post was an empty packing-case on the top deck of the two-story poop ; the two *amahs* squatted behind her. Her orders to the captain were given directly, or if he was too far away to hear to one of the *amahs*, who immediately jumped down from her monkey-like position and ran to fetch him. She never spoke to any of the crew, nor did the *amahs*. Occasionally the captain asked her something, and she always replied very curtly and almost haughtily.

After all, she *did* rule supreme. She was the owner of eleven other junks, all bristling with cannons, rifles and pistols. There were no machine-guns.*

---

* Though none of Lai Choi San's ships carried this deadly weapon, some of the other pirate clans along the West River do have war canoes equipped with machine-guns both fore and aft. These weapons are doubtless property stolen from the Chinese army.

The haze had now disappeared altogether, but dark clouds were piling up on the horizon. It probably meant rain squalls and strong winds. The captain gazed in the direction of the approaching clouds, and, turning to me, said in pidgin-English : " Much lain, much wind come byebye, maybe go way."

In the meantime, right above us, the sun was shining brightly, and the air was very clear. Ideal weather for a photographer, and what a subject to photograph.

The moment Lai Choi San saw my magic box she rebelled. She gave an order to the captain, who approached and told me to put away the kodak.

That was where I rebelled.

I told him to go back to this pirate woman and tell her that since I was paying a good deal of money for the privilege of sailing with her I proposed to take as many pictures as I liked. If I was not to be allowed to do so, the whole trip would be a failure so far as I was concerned, and they might just as well put me ashore.

A hot half an hour of parleying followed, but finally she smiled graciously at me and I smiled back at her. I told Moon to go to her and ask if I might take her picture. I expected an outburst of indignation, but nothing like that happened. On the contrary, she agreed to pose. Oh, you inconsistent women !

Then the captain came, and with Moon interpreting we thoroughly discussed the problem of future photography on board the junk. In short, we agreed that I should not take pictures of anything of an incriminating nature. Incriminating nature ! Could anything sound more unpromising to the ears of a journalist ?

*   *   *   *   *

That same afternoon our adventures began.

The horizon was dotted with the black sails of myriads of junks composing the fishing-fleets. Behind and above them hovered those dark rain clouds which blew ever eastward but never reached us. We sailed to the leeward of an island and out of sight of the on-coming junks. Within an hour the first ships were in line with our island; then we emerged from our hiding-place.

Madame gave a sharp order. She had singled out a large black junk with three yellow sails gleaming brightly in the sunshine. We sailed towards this ship, which was apparently heavily laden with fish. As soon as the junk recognized us it turned and fled, but we rapidly overtook it. Our crew had brought out the rifles and had put on cartridge belts, and so had Madame and both of her *amahs*. When we were within hearing distance of the fleeing junk one of our men fired a rifle shot. I was certain that the junk would fight, and was already wondering where I might hide myself from bullets or other missiles which would soon be flying about our deck, but nothing occurred.

A second shot was fired, and the junk's mainsail came down. We sailed up and hove to a short distance from her.

Forgetting Madame's request that I refrain from taking photographs of an " incriminating nature," I was ready to " shoot " a real battle scene. Here again I was disappointed, because nothing really exciting happened. A man on the poop of the other junk shouted something through a megaphone. Our skipper yelled back at him in a volley of rapid Chinese which I could not understand. Then a dinghy was lowered from the other ship, and the " enemy " captain came over.

Long before he reached our ship we could see him gesticulating wildly, and as soon as he was within hearing distance he began to jabber away excitedly. He was highly nervous, and as soon as he came aboard us he was taken below to the captain's quarters. Quite a while afterwards he again appeared, smiling broadly, and soon he was returning to his ship. Apparently the business had been settled to the satisfaction of everyone concerned.

While all these incidents were taking place Madame had continued to sit with her two *amahs* at her observation post, silent and unmoved as though she were utterly oblivious of what was going on. Whether she did this deliberately in order to deceive the onlookers on board the other ship, or whether such an attitude was her " second nature," I am unable to say. However, judging from my later experiences while " adventuring " with her, I believe the latter to be the case.

The captain seemed highly pleased with the enemy's visit, and I wondered how much money it had netted him.

These formalities completed, we sailed away in search of new victims. Two more junks were chased in a like manner, but they struck sail immediately after the first signal shot was fired. Their captains paid similar visits to our ship, and each time the captain's smile became broader and broader. He was highly elated and even jocular.

Anxious to know what the profits of the day had been, I shouted: " Hey, captain, feeling top-side ? Makee plentee money " ?

And he replied: " Sure ! Plentee money makee heart light."

She will not escape

Pursuit

The captain—" this Chinaman "

" Chow ": meal-time on board Lai Choi San's ship

We spent the night at anchor to leeward of an island. One of the *amahs* lighted a bunch of incense sticks and placed them in various parts of the ship. This was a tribute to any gods who might have the power to send a happy ending to the day.

The trip thus far had been rather exciting; I was tired, and suddenly I realized that I was very hungry. Moon offered to fry a chicken, and I encouraged him to go and do so. Some of the men went away in the dinghy to spear fish by torchlight; I went with them, but soon returned to the ship—I was too hungry to stay away from the smell of that cooking chicken. Moon spread a napkin on the deck to serve as a tablecloth, and as if by magic he got hold of a number of European utensils —whence I never knew.

When I was ready to begin the feast Madame appeared, and I gallantly asked her to taste the chicken. She took both legs and most of the white meat, and declared that she liked it very much. She was a pirate all right! I whispered to Moon that, should the men return with a good catch, he was to grab most of it to retaliate for her greediness.

*   *   *   *   *

Shortly before daylight we weighed anchor and sailed off again. To the east and northward high mountains were turning blue, and a few scattered sails could be seen along the horizon to the south.

The captain invited me to have breakfast with him, and the crew gathered round, roaring at my ridiculous manœuvres with the chopsticks. I should have remained hungry had not Madame ordered Moon to bring me my fork and spoon.

The women always dined separately from the men. The captain ate with the crew, and all fared alike.

About eleven o'clock we struck a calm. There was nothing for the crew to do but sit around and chatter, and so the captain and I had time to become friendly. He told me a great deal about Madame's business and her methods of procedure.

As an " inspector " it was her duty to sail from one fishing fleet to another and see that no harm should come to them from pirates. If a hostile junk was accosted it was the inspector's business to chase the pirate away, and if necessary fight him, sink the ship, and capture the crew. Consequently, in order to be successful, she must be strong enough to hold her own with any kind of antagonists. This meant that the larger the ship and the more cannons it carried the better chance the inspector had to sit on the top of the piratical world.

Every junk had to pay tribute to the inspector. If it did not pay—why, occasionally accidents happened, and not infrequently did non-payers disappear. There were also other " inspector " junks hanging about and levying taxes on the fishing fleet when Madame was not around, and thus the helpless fisherfolk usually paid tribute to several inspectors in order to prevent trouble. Lately, however, a few of these smaller fry had decided to consolidate themselves into a stronger fleet and drive Madame out of business. This, at least, was rumoured, according to the captain.

Lai Choi San, being a good general, decided to stop all of these plans of her competitors while the stopping was easy. With a fair wind and barring accident, she hoped to reach an island that day where she knew several competing junks were harboured, and there talk matters over with their captains. Surely enough, within a few hours I had a wonderful occasion to witness Madame's rather unscrupulous methods of "talking matters over."

About noon a breeze sprang up, our sails filled, the mast creaked, the junk heeled over under the bellying canvas, and we sailed along steadily until we reached a hilly island heavily covered with vegetation. There, in a small bay, three junks rode at anchor. As soon as they sighted us two of them hoisted their sails and started to move away.

The captain rushed over to me.

"You go down!"

It was an order to go below. I refused; but a few husky, slant - eyed gentlemen closed in upon me and pushed me, not too gently, in the direction of the open hatch, by way of emphasizing the captain's unquestionable authority. So below I went, and a moment later Moon rolled down to keep me company. The pirates most assuredly meant business.

The cabin was dark. A few rays of light found their way through a crack in the closed hatch. We could hear the crew running up and down the deck and shouting. I wondered what was going to happen, and if there was going to be a battle. Suppose there should be an old-fashioned hand-to-hand encounter; in that case my position would not be enviable. I had the uncomfortable feeling that in the event of the ship foundering I should find myself trapped.

"Moon, what do you think is going to happen?" I asked, more to hear his voice than in the hope of getting any reassuring information.

"No savee, master."

D

As he spoke the whole junk shook from a salvo from our guns. The noise was deafening.

Boom! There went another! And a third, a fourth, a fifth and a sixth! A regular bombardment—but there were no reply shots. The enemy probably never got a chance to fire back. It was indeed a one-sided affair.

The nauseous smell of burnt black powder reached us down below. Then I heard more shouting and many rifle shots, apparently fired by our own people. I realized that if the other junk should return our fire my prison would not be particularly safe. I lay down flat upon the deck, hiding my head behind the base of the mast. But there were no return shots from the attacked party.

After a while I sat up and tried, as calmly as possible, to talk Moon into believing that there was really no danger at all, and that our whole trip was a wonderful picnic. I was grateful for the fact that the cabin was too dark for him to see the expression on my face.

Still, we sat there for at least an hour, during which time we had an opportunity for some thinking, perhaps a bit of praying, and much swearing, all of which resulted in a sufficiency of resolutions to be good in the future.

Then the hatch was opened and I was allowed to come up on deck.

The first thing I saw was two men bound hand and foot. Some distance away to starboard I saw the sinking hull of the junk. Without asking permission I put my camera into vigorous action.

I saw on the poop Her Majesty, the Queen of Pirates, sitting on her throne-like box with her attendants behind her. They wore cartridge belts around their waists and held rifles in their hands, but, curiously enough, they

" The first thing I saw was two men bound hand and foot "

" Some distance to starboard I saw the sinking hull of the junk "

A dragon procession at a Chinese wedding (*p.* 56)

offered no objection to posing for me in this piratical uniform.

I asked the captain who the two prisoners were. He replied with a snarl that they were the two captains with whom Madame had " talked matters over." Quite a forceful way of parleying, I thought ; still, this was South China—and the Kingdom of the Pirates. I asked the captain if I might photograph the prisoners, and attend the execution in the event of their being shot.

Of course, I could take as many pictures as I liked, but those men would probably not be shot, he whispered. Most likely they would be exchanged for heavy cash. If you shoot an enemy there is always a lot of explaining to do, and all sorts of authorities and relatives to pacify ; but if you keep him for a certain period bound hand and foot, and occasionally let him go hungry for a few days, cash is almost certain to be forthcoming. And there is practically no danger.

I asked him how he knew that the relatives would pay up. He smiled. In this case it was an easy matter ; he would simply deliver the prisoners to their villages, and the townsmen would pay cold cash to the amount of several hundred dollars per head. Yes, this was a rather easy matter to handle. It was hardly a case of kidnapping. Sometimes when a messenger was sent to the relatives they did not believe that a prisoner was really being held for ransom ; and sometimes, again, relatives did not care to ransom the prisoners, hoping against hope that the captive would be killed, and that they would inherit all his wealth. But those cases were rare. It was after the third or fourth demand for ransom money that the prisoner's ear, or a finger, or a hand was chopped off and delivered with a message that next time some other part of his body would accompany the chit. Finally, if the money was definitely refused—well—it was just bad luck for the poor victim.

A dinghy was lowered, the prisoners were helped to their feet, carried on board the dinghy, and then rowed away. I wanted to go with them, just to see what their fate would be, and to witness the actual bargaining over the ransom, but I was not allowed to do so. The captain himself was in command of the dinghy. When they returned a couple of hours later he wore a satisfied expression, and so did the crew. Later I actually saw the captain show Lai Choi San a fat roll of bills.

It was on this second day that Madame first permitted me to ask her a few questions. I believe that she had a hard time trying to overcome her distrust of me. Occasionally she had deigned to smile somewhere in my direction, but I had not once heard her laugh loudly until, quite unexpectedly, one of the large muzzle-loading cannons was accidentally discharged close behind me, and I jumped a few feet in the air, almost scared out of my wits. That was the only time that I saw her really merry.

The sea was getting rough and our junk began to pitch uncomfortably, though not enough to make me seasick. She wondered why, so I told her that I was used to the sea, having been reared in a country where there are thousands of lakes, and where every youngster is born practically a seaman. She wondered where that could be. I told her in Finland. She wanted to know where that country was—in America? So I drew a crude map of the world, and tried to describe as well as I could through my interpreter the shape of the earth and the whereabouts of " Melica, Inliss and Faranca "—respectively America, England and France. Slowly we crept up to such indescribable places as the Scandinavian countries, and finally we came to Finland. There, I said, on the opposite side of the earth, was the spot where I was born.

How far was it from Canton? A two, three day sailing—with a fair wind?

Then and there I gave up for ever my career as a teacher of Chinese women pirates.

Presently she told me a little more about her early life.

Her father had had four sons, but they were all dead. She had been his only daughter, and being a frail and delicate child had not been expected to live. Her father used to take her with him on his trips along the coast, regarding her more as a servant than as a child of his own. And now she loved the sea.

The old man had started his life penniless, as a mere coolie, but he had had a remarkable career for all that. He had been a brave lad, and probably ruthless. He got into the good graces of a brigand chief, whose haunts were somewhere along the West River. This chieftain made him his Number One man, and when a few years later the old bandit died " unexpectedly " the Number One man proclaimed himself chief. And so he took possession of a few junks and went on the warpath against the neighbouring pirates, whom he drove out of their strongholds. Thus he became respected and feared among the seafaring merchantmen along the South China coast, made a goodly amount of money, and collected junks as one collects stamps or Chinese porcelain. He acquired a large fleet, but some of the ships foundered and some were burned by treacherous crews; but the fishing junks—several hundreds of them—each paid him a certain amount of money as long as he guaranteed that no other pirate would harass them in their lawful pursuit of livelihood.

When he died, with " his slippers on," from wounds received during the encounter which my friend, the American in Macao, had told me about, he left Lai Choi San seven ships, the strongest and largest on the waters of the West and Pearl Rivers. She also attested that she had " acquired " a few more, and that to-day she actually owns twelve large armoured junks.

She is rich, probably rich beyond comprehension. She owns a house in Macao which she occupies occasionally, but her home is in one of the villages on the West River.

" What do the words Lai Choi San mean ? " I asked Moon.

He said that Madame would have to write down the characters of her name. He could not tell me unless he saw them. I asked her to write her name on a piece of paper.

She glared at me. I believe that she strongly suspected a trap, or some other devilry. She did not want to do it. Finally, I asked my interpreter whether he thought that she knew how to write. He translated this to her. The trick worked. Scorning to answer my question, she snatched the proferred pencil and laboriously wrote the three characters.

Lai Choi San, *The Mountain of Wealth*. Not an unfitting, although not exactly a feminine name. Still, her career was not very feminine either.

Had she no ambitions to settle down to a peaceful life ? I asked. Why did she continue this dangerous business ?

Moon translated the question, and she replied with a shrug. She probably could not think of an answer.

But I think I know it. The trade of buccaneering,

" He was a real little man and a brave chap " [54

The heir to Lai Choi San's wealth and trade

in one form or another, is actually in the blood of the South China coast people. These hills, these rocky islands and waters, have for centuries been their territory, by right or might. When the plucky Portuguese arrived in the fifteenth century they immediately declared war on the brigands, and Macao was handed over to them by the Son of Heaven as a token of appreciation for what they did to suppress the activities of the marauders. The Chinese authorities, Imperial or Republican, have never been strong enough to cope with the situation, and the Portuguese of Macao, or the Hong - Kong British of to-day, cannot very well start any punitive expeditions of their own on foreign territory.

Would she not rather settle down and marry? Have children?

Moon for some reason made an attempt to wriggle out of this question. But I understood enough Cantonese to force him back into the right track, and stammering, he finally asked the question.

It did not seem to be a matter of etiquette with her. I had no idea at the time that she had been married twice, that her first husband had gone to his ancestors after a short and lively dispute over a trivial domestic matter —how and when I did not venture to ask her. Her second husband " had not been really her husband," she told me through Moon. But for all that, she had had many lovers.

Had she any children?

She certainly had, she said proudly. Two boys. One was in Shanghai, where a relative had put him in the school. This boy was the son of her first husband. He was twenty now, and a fine boy. He was going to marry the only daughter of the richest man in Shekki, a neighbouring town of Macao. The young people had been engaged since early childhood. There would be a wonderful wedding with a dragon procession, and all the presents would be carried on lacquered trays along the streets of the city. There would be many, many dollars' worth of fire-crackers burned, too, and she would give him rich gifts of money, and her house in Macao to live in.

Did she not want him to take up her own "trade"? I ventured to remark.

Oh, no! She wanted him to become a rich rice merchant and to go to Mei Kwo, which is Chinese for America, and see the wonderful country she had heard so much about. She had once seen in an old newspaper a picture of the fantastically tall buildings of a strange city, and someone had said that all the cities in Mei Kwo had similar buildings. She wanted him to go there, sell rice to the foreign people, and get himself a building like those she had seen in the paper. But she did not want him to sail up and down the rivers looking for loot, although if he stayed in Macao he could probably acquire the *fan-tan* concession there eventually. It would not be so bad, either.

But the second son? What about him?

He was a child yet, she said, only five years old. He was going to be a sailor all right. He was already in training on another of her junks. One day he was going to inherit all her ships and the "trade." He was a real little man, she explained, and a brave chap. He smoked like a man too. She did not want him to sail with *her* on her ship; it was better that he should stay away from his mother. But whenever the junks were in harbour at any of the islands she always had him brought over.

I had Moon ask her : Was this chap, too, the son of her first husband ?

She admitted that he was not. He was a real love child.

I did not pursue the question farther.

It struck me that I should get her ideas on the eternal question of Love, a Chinese woman pirate's view of it.

This time Moon did not giggle or try to evade the question. He was keenly interested himself. But Madame would not answer. She gave a long, searching look first at Moon and then at me, realizing that I was the originator of the question. And then, for the first time, I read sadness in her eyes.

She did not answer my question.

*　　　*　　　*　　　*　　　*

We anchored that night in the shelter of the cape which divides Mirs Bay from Bias Bay. For reasons of his own the captain extinguished all the lights, and our food was cooked over charcoal below deck. It was a very uncomfortable night. Mosquitoes sang their arias in my ears throughout the night ; there was not the slightest breeze to blow them away.

Next morning, about half an hour before sunrise, a bit of wind came along and we again set sail. At last we were cruising up Bias Bay. The country around was hilly and unfriendly. The weather became stormy, with occasional rain squalls. A few junks hovered near the shore, and a small village appeared through the haze to the right.

The bay is very shallow, and we anchored a mile or so from the shore.

It was understood that I was going ashore to pay a visit to the principal village of Fan Lo Kong. Naturally I asked the captain if he were not coming along to see his uncle, who, according to him, was living in Fan Lo Kong. He shook his head and mumbled something which I did not understand, and busied himself with something of no importance. He would not come along —not this time—but he would let me have as many men as I wanted for a bodyguard. I suggested that I take five men, three to go with me, and two to watch the boat.

A dinghy went overboard, and then the men rowed Moon and me for a little while ; but soon the water became too shallow for rowing, and they all jumped out and pulled the boat along. They would not let me wade ; I had to stay in the boat. Meantime I studied a sketch map which had been given to me by a native member of the Hong-Kong Police Force who had once been in Bias Bay as a spy. I was very anxious to photograph a house which he had told me of, where all prisoners were kept while their ransoms were being negotiated, and where many people had been tortured and murdered when ransom had not been forthcoming. According to the sketch it was a comparatively small house. I expected to find it on the other side of the village, not very far from the main street.

We landed near a group of small houses, where we were met by a few old men, women, and children. All the young men had disappeared. My ruffians went rummaging in the houses, and for some reason, even to-day not clear to me, they entered one house and came out dragging a small boy who held a baby in his arms. I protested against molesting any of the children, and

They took me ashore

The landing party in Bias Bay

" We were met by a few old men, women and children "

they finally let the frightened, crying youngster go, but not until he had set up a healthy clamour. This overture was not at all to my liking. It would give the inhabitants an idea that our intentions were hostile, an impression that I was extremely anxious to avoid giving them. I hastened to present the still sobbing boy with a few silver coins ; then we marched off towards the village, which was located about a mile from the shore. This was the same village which the British had partly destroyed in March, 1927, following an especially atrocious piracy. Though they had demolished over one hundred houses, and had blown up and burned about forty junks, they had only succeeded in demonstrating the futility of such reprisals, for within two months a new piracy had been added to the bloody record of Bias Bay, and before the end of the year there were many more.

*   *   *   *   *

So this was Bias Bay !

I had heard a great deal of " The Nest," but to me it looked like any other Chinese village, with huts and houses, and walls around the gardens, and the usual domestic zoo of pigs, dogs, and multitudes of ready-plucked poultry taking up every inch of the road. There were, of course, the children, the beggars, and the screeching " honey " carts which spread an infernal smell wherever they passed.

Although it had been raining hard, numerous babies were sitting in the middle of the road black with mud. Only upon seeing our approach did their mothers rush out in the road, grab the children and then run madly away. Some women behind heavily-barred windows and doorways shouted curses at us.

They saw me, a foreigner, enter the village with a strange-looking thing, the camera, in my hand, surrounded by half-naked, armed men as a bodyguard. I am certain that they took me for a British official, or policeman, and they had every reason to hate the British, the only people who had ever dared to meddle with their alleged trade rights as pirates, a heritage from time immemorial.

A honking flock of geese fled down the road in front of us with outstretched necks and flapping wings; a black cat crossed the road and darted up a tree; then the rain began in earnest.

We marched along the main street straight up to the house that I wanted to photograph. It was a corner house which lent itself very well to photography. The light was so bad that it was necessary to make a time exposure. I could hear a woman's squeaky voice inside the house, occasionally interrupted by a man's harsh jabber. A dog barked furiously and once something banged loudly. Then there was complete silence.

Moon had handed me the tripod, and I mounted the camera to make the exposure. Meantime my men had taken shelter from the rain behind the wall around the house. I was just ready to press the bulb when a door in the wall opened and an angry Chinese came out, shaking his fist at me and advancing rapidly toward my camera. My men grabbed their rifles and ran to my assistance, still unobserved by the enraged householder. I have never seen anyone turn round so quickly and bolt back to shelter as this man did when he saw my approaching protectors. The door slammed behind him, and we all had a good laugh.

Meantime several scores of villagers had assembled

at a safe distance away, where they stood observing us. I had travelled in China long enough to become accustomed to such demonstrations of native curiosity, but I did not like the threatening silence which this mob of youngsters and half-grown men and women maintained. When we moved away they moved too ; when we stopped they stopped. I looked them over and decided that a show of boldness was the safe policy. So I strode down the street, paying no more attention to the mob than I should have done to a group of children.

The rain had stopped, but the road was slippery ; one of my men fell into the mud, and the crowd set up a chatter of Chinese sarcasm.

I did not see any temples, but there were a few " joss-houses " and the usual open stores, such as one finds in all Chinese villages. There was no sound of music or song, and the impression we received was gloomy. But I wanted to make the rounds of the village, so we marched on to the very centre of the maze of narrow, malodorous streets that are Fan Lo Kong.

It was a good half hour before we finally returned to the road which led down to the Bay. There is an open place where this road reaches the village, and here several hundred more persons had assembled. They were expecting us ; that was evident. Their attitude was not friendly. They threw sarcastic remarks at us, but they made no move to attack us. I told Moon to order the men not to answer their remarks nor to do anything which might provoke any unfriendly move. My men closed about me. I could see their fingers toying with the breech mechanism of their rifles as we passed through the throng. Something was bound to happen.

Some of the women called out to us in vile language.

Then the first stone came flying. It missed us and splashed in the mud a yard or so away. The man in front of me swung around, but I pushed him ahead. A few more stones were thrown at us, and still nothing serious happened. I began to hope that we could make our way through the mob without any accidents occurring.

Then someone hurled another stone, hitting one of my men on the right shoulder. Roaring with rage, he whirled, threw his rifle to his shoulder, and pointed it to the crowd. Yelling, the throng fled in all directions, the children stumbling against each other and the men and women throwing themselves on the ground. Indescribable confusion followed. I expected to hear the crack from the rifle, but to my great relief there was only a sharp click, and I knew the rifle had missed fire.

Thank God !

I grabbed the man's gun, pushed it aside, and told him to go ahead and behave himself. We reached the road without further adventures.

We had yet to walk about a mile before reaching our boat. The crowd followed along after us until we reached the shore. I stepped into the boat, the men waded alongside, pushing it through the shallow water. Then the fun began. We made a first-class target there on the open water, and the good people of Bias Bay were soon amusing themselves by laying down a regular barrage, in front, behind, and all around us. But they were poor marksmen, or else we were lucky. We passed through it without a scratch.

It was with relief that I found myself safe again aboard our pirate junk. The first to greet me was the captain. He had, of course, heard the shots, and he

Ransacking houses in Bias Bay

The House of Torture, Fan Lo Kong, Bias Bay   [62

The water front of Macao

Macao—street of disrepute

intimated that he had been on the point of sending a rescue party for us.

"Well, captain," I questioned, "aren't you going to visit your uncle in Bias Bay?"

"No," he said. "No, I no think my uncle likee me. I think he shootee me if he see me. No, my uncle not likee me at all."

  *   *   *   *   *

Two days later I was back in Hong-Kong. The junk had taken me as far as the south shore of the island, and from there I had walked all the way to the city of Victoria itself. Lai Choi San had refused to sail into the harbour. Her armed junks were not welcome there I understood.

On reaching the city I again met my old friend, Chang Liu, as he was emerging from the Hong-Kong and Shanghai Bank. He came directly up to me.

"So you are back from Bias Bay?"

As a matter of fact I had been in town exactly one hour and twenty-five minutes; yet he already knew that I had been to Bias Bay.

"Yes," I boasted, "and as you see, nothing has happened to me. And if you will come up to my hotel in a day or two I shall be glad to show you the photographs I have taken."

"Well, my friend," he said, "I have a suggestion to make. I am a friend of yours, and I should hate to see anything happen to you, but if you continue your so-called 'investigation' something is bound to happen."

"Chang Liu, is this a friendly warning, or are you threatening me?"

"As you like. But let us have lunch together."

So we went for luncheon to the Hong-Kong Hotel.

"Look here, Chang," I said, "let us have an under-

standing.   You realize that I have travelled 10,000 miles
to make ' copy ' out of you and your kind . . . "

"What do you mean, ' you and your kind ' ? "

"Well, I have found out about you," I continued,
" but I give you my word that your secrets are not going
to be disclosed to anybody. I like you. If you wish to
help me, I shall greatly appreciate it. If you don't—
well and good. If you don't interfere with me, I promise
to leave you alone. If you want to hear about yourself,
I shall be glad to let you have it right now."

Then I unloaded all of my suspicions as I had
constructed them in my mind from the documents which
the Colonial Secretary had permitted me to peep into. I
told him that he probably was one of those " higher-ups "
who organized and instigated the high-seas piracies which
the Bias Bay ruffians were paid to execute. And I also
told him my reasons for believing that most of the high-seas
piracies were engineered by him, or by men like him.

Chang Liu had put down his knife and fork, and sat
staring at me in a bewildered manner.

"Who has told you all of this rot ? " he demanded
at last. " If you think you have discovered something,
you are grossly mistaken."

"By the way," I said, " have you ever seen this
document ? "

I handed him a circular letter which the Hong-Kong
police had sent in May, 1929, to all shipping offices,
and caused to be broadcast to ships at sea. It read as
follows :—

Hong - Kong police have received the following
information :—

1. The pirates named below left Wong Fau on the
twenty-fourth day of the third moon (3rd May, 1929) and

walked to Siu Mok, which is 30 li away, and from there they engaged a boat to go to Swatow. They stayed in a boarding house at Chung Pong Street near the New Road and Garden Road, Swatow. They held a meeting at the Kam Kee Tea House near the To Toi Yamun and decided to go to Singapore. They should soon arrive at Singapore, where they will take up their lodgings at the Tak Kee Boarding House at Ngau Che Shui.

2. Yeung Fok, 30, having two gold teeth in the upper front jaw, native of Sheung Yeung Wai Village, Wai Chau.

Yeung Pat, 30, having gold tooth in lower front jaw, native of Sheung Yeung Wai Village, Wai Chau.

Chau Ah So, 40, having two gold teeth in the upper front jaw, native of Pak Sha Pao, Ping Shan.

Chau Ah Choi, 30, native of Pak Sha Pao Village, Ping Shan.

Ting Ah San, 20, native of Pak Mong Fa, Wai Chau.

Chan Ah Cheung, 30, having two gold teeth in the upper front jaw, native of Pak Mong Fa, Wai Chau.

Chung Tin Si, 30, native of San Ok Chai Village, Fan Wo Kong.

Chung Ah Sing, 40, native of San Ok Chai Village, Fan Wo Kong.

Lam Koon Ting, 40, native of San Ok Chai Village, Fan Wo Kong.

Lam Choi, 40, native of San Ok Chai Village, Fan Wo Kong.

Chan Wye, 30, having two gold teeth in the upper front jaw, native of Pak Mong Fa, Wai Chau.

Chang Liu read the document and laughed.

" These names of gold-jawed gentlemen," he cried,

E

" are all invented. I know pretty well every inhabitant of the villages around Bias Bay . . . "

Then he caught himself. He looked at me strangely.

" I think you have made me talk too much."

This was his first real admission that he knew anything about the pirates of Bias Bay.*

The circular letter I had handed him had been given me by the Hong-Kong police ; however, I suspected that it had been manufactured by an " informant " among the Bias Bay pirates themselves in order to mislead the police. It may be noted that there is no Tak Kee boarding-house on Ngau Che Shui in Singapore, as I later learned from personal investigation in that city.

" Look here, Chang Liu," I said, " do you really think that the British will tolerate a hornets' nest like Bias

---

* There is a ruthless war going on between the Hong-Kong police and the Bias Bay pirates. It is characterized by espionage, counter-espionage, betrayals, shooting affrays, bribery, double-crossing, and now and then enlivened by the audacious piracy of an ocean-going ship. Superficially, it would seem that the Hong-Kong authorities could easily crush these pirates, and blow Bias Bay with all its villages and strongholds to pieces. But, theoretically at least, the British cannot very well start punitive expeditions against the pirates without infringing upon Chinese sovereignty. Theoretically they cannot, but in actual practice they have been forced to do so, because the Chinese authorities have openly admitted their inability to do anything to relieve an intolerable situation. They have consistently refused to co-operate in any effort to punish these murderous desperadoes. Indeed, upon one occasion they have even had the audacity to request that the British should not disturb the Bias Bay gangs, because any move against them might result in further reprisals. This happened in March, 1927, after the pirates had committed a new outrage against the British shipping, and in reply to the Hong-Kong Government's formal request that the Chinese authorities take immediate steps to apprehend and

Bay almost within the reach of their guns ? Don't you
think that one day they are going to ship their troops
over to Bias Bay and blow the whole country to pieces ? "

He gave me a queer look, shrugged his shoulders, and
said curtly : " Well, why don't they ? "

That was all I got out of him.

A few minutes later he excused himself and shook
hands with me ; then we parted, only to meet again
months later under most dramatic circumstances.

*   *   *   *   *

The trip on Lai Choi San's pirate junk had been
something of a " glorious adventure." The tropical heat
of Hong-Kong was again becoming too oppressive, and
I longed to return to the wide, foamy spaces, where

punish the bandits guilty of the crime, which had been committed
outside British jurisdiction, the Chinese made this suggestion.

Mr. Eugene Chen, the Jamaica-born Chinese leader, at that
time the head of the Hankow Government, actually gave Mr.
Erich Teichmann, of the British Legation, the advice to leave
the pirates alone. This was too much for Great Britain, and
the Hong-Kong authorities decided to attend to the matters
themselves.

On the very day that Mr. Teichmann had transmitted Mr.
Chen's suggestion to Hong-Kong the British sent three hundred
men in seventeen launches to Bias Bay ; they landed, burned
or blew up forty junks, and destroyed one hundred and thirty
houses. I had seen the ruins during my visit to Bias Bay.

The Hankow Government did not feel in the least ashamed
or apologetic because of their inability to handle the situation,
and it is interesting to note that, on the contrary, they turned
this purely punitive expedition of the British into red-hot anti-
foreign propaganda. Posters were displayed throughout China
depicting the British as " murdering over one thousand men,
women and children, bombarding and burning whole villages
on Chinese territory, etc."

pirate junks have their rendezvous, and where the freebooter is a noble man.   I had not heard anything from Chang Liu since we had parted at the luncheon in the Hong-Kong Hotel.   Otherwise, I should have pestered him to come along with me on a second trip to Bias Bay.   I should have liked to make a trip with him as my guide, because he undoubtedly knew all the bandits personally, as well as their haunts, their secrets, and their methods of doing business.

Again I sought the Earless One. He was standing before the door as usual, but he smelled of opium and looked groggy.

"Hey, Earless One," I called, "have you been in heaven ? "

"Just come down, master. Just come down," he chuckled, steering me inside the shop. "Wantee buy more jade ? "

"No, wantee see Chang Liu."

"Solly, Chang Liu gone East."

"East ? How far East ? To Bias Bay ? "

At this moment I saw a figure move in the doorway. It was a white man, and at first I could not recognize his face against the sharp light outside ; but the Earless One cringed, and then I saw that the new-comer was a member of the Hong-Kong police force.   He knew, of course, who I was ; and it probably was to show off his knowledge that he said :

"Still looking for pirates ? You won't find out anything from this bird. We have had him up time and again. If you can, you are luckier than we are."

What an ass this man was ! What would the Earless One think of me now ? Doubtless, that I was in league with the police or Government agents.

The Macao fishing-fleet

Fish laid out to dry—Macao

There is gambling in every temple yard in Macao (*p.* 77)

" Well, sergeant," I said rather sharply, " suppose you go about your own business and I will follow my own methods. You are working for the police ; I am not. You are an enemy of these fellows ; I wish to be their *friend*."

He looked at me with a sarcastic smile wrinkling his freckled face.

" Friend ! A good friend you are ! You hang around these chaps and then print cock - and - bull stories about them—and what do the police get out of it ? Nothing ! Just become a laughing - stock to thousands of people all over the world."

" Thanks for the compliment. I wish you had said millions of people. I hope my stories will be read by so many. . . ."

" Go on and hope ! And, by the way, the chief would like to know how long you are going to stay in Hong-Kong."

" Why this sudden interest in my person ? Are you people afraid I will find out too much about you and what you have been doing with piracies, or rather what you have *not* been doing ? Tell your chief that when I am ready to go I will go."

He slammed the door and strode off down the street.

This was my first unpleasant experience with the Hong-Kong police, but I had achieved my purpose of giving the Earless One the impression that this police-sergeant and I were not friends. Subsequently he loosened up ; then more tea was served, and I stayed in the little shop all that forenoon.

The Earless One told me that if I could get into the Hong-Kong Prison and interview a few men, comparatively short-time prisoners—three years—in the jail, I could gather a lot of information. He gave me the name of one man who was probably a squealer and a double-crosser, and assured me that if I could see him and talk with him it would be a good thing for *me*. He intimated that this man might be able to give me startling information. He also told me that Chang Liu could give me the names of more of them, if he wished to do so, and he even agreed to speak to Chang Liu about it.

I went to the Peninsula Hotel and had lunch with one of the minor officials connected with the Colonial Secretary's Office. He had been of great assistance to me on other occasions, but when I brought up the subject of arranging an interview with some of the Chinese prisoners he was horrified.

"But," he suggested, "why not see the defence lawyers ? Perhaps the matter could be arranged through them."

He offered to find out which firm had conducted the defence of the bandits I wished to see, provided that I would give him the names of the prisoners.

This was a clumsy trap. Any pirate brought to justice by the Hong - Kong authorities is hanged. Consequently these pirates had been imprisoned for minor offences without the authorities knowing that they were pirates. Suppose, therefore, that I should mention their names to this official. The result would be disastrous for the convicts. The Earless One had given me certain information which was highly important to me. If I could get at the truth of the Bias Bay piracies, if I could get the prisoners to talk, and especially if I could get them to mention names of the " higher-ups," what " copy " it would make. I had no intention of spoiling it in order to do the authorities a favour.

Later in the evening I went to see the Earless One, and we talked the matter over rather seriously. He was now convinced that I was not a policeman, and that I had not co-operated in any way with the enemies of the men of Bias Bay, because as soon as I had left the store in the morning two Chinese detectives had come in and cross-examined him concerning his dealings with me. A lucky stroke!

The next thing was to go back to the Colonial Secretary's Office and find out whether or not I would be permitted to interview the prisoners in Victoria Jail. The officials were at first mildly astonished, but when I refused to promise to divulge whatever I might learn they were irritated. One very dignified looking secretary told me what I had heard so often before; namely, that journalists were nuisances, and should not be allowed to live.

*   *   *   *   *

That evening I spent alone on the spacious veranda of the hotel with Hong-Kong's myriads of lights twinkling against the black hills above me like a million stars. I meditated upon a means of getting into Victoria Jail. One way would be to get drunk and drive an automobile down the street on the wrong side of the traffic, get myself arrested, and if only fined, give the dignified judge a lot of saucy lip work. Another way would be to shop-lift a pair of pyjamas. After all, there were many ways.

Somebody tapped me on the shoulder. It was a friend of mine who was one of the American Consular officials.

"Why so lonely? Dreaming about the girl you left behind?"

"Hell, no! I am meditating on how to get into jail."

"That is easy enough. Write a bad cheque and in you will go, or sign a lot of chits and don't pay for them, or beat your hotel bill, or get into a fight, or steal a lady's purse, or . . . as you see, there are many ways. But why get into jail here? Don't do that. You know, we have been seen together a great deal."

"I want to get hold of some men now in jail."

"Too bad, too bad." He looked at me dubiously. "What devilry have you been up to? Why do you wish to get into trouble?"

This was the Consular official who spoke to me now—not my friend.

"I am just planning what devilry could send me to jail, and as you have suggested many ways I shall, after careful consideration, decide which of the wrong paths of life I will follow. And later I'll blame it all on you."

He excused himself suddenly and hurried away.

*   *   *   *   *

I could not sleep that night. It was hot, and two rickshaw boys on the street outside spent several hours discussing the domestic difficulties of somebody else. I wanted to take a cold bath, but there was no water running. Hong-Kong was at that time suffering from the worst drought in twenty-five years. Then and there I decided to go back to Macao, get in touch with Lai Choi San and her crew, and go along with them for days or weeks, if the matter could be arranged.

The first person I met on the water-front of Macao

was "this Chinaman." I asked him to come up to my hotel, where I could show him the pictures I had taken during our trip to Bias Bay. I have seldom seen any Chinese so enthusiastic as he was when he saw his own likeness grinning up at him. After I had shown him all the pictures, I told him that I expected to give a copy of each of them to Lai Choi San.

He grinned and made a gesture.

Oh, she was not in Macao now. She was in Canton, maybe not in Canton itself, but somewhere between Canton and Macao; maybe not there, but farther over towards West River. After all, he wasn't certain she was even there.

I saw through his game. He wanted those pictures, and he wanted them badly. He knew that if this was the only set of pictures I had Lai Choi San would keep them all and he would get nothing. So he preferred to lay hands on the photographs first, and some time later let the old lady see whatever pictures he wanted to part with. I gave him all the photographs and told him that I would have another set for Lai Choi San. Then I asked when she would be back in Macao. He replied that he expected her in a few weeks, but then she might not come at all.

I decided to wait for her arrival. Meantime I would give Macao a thorough "look-see."

PART TWO

UNTIL about one hundred years ago Macao was an important commercial city, so important that both the Dutch and the British coveted it, and the Chinese wished it returned to them. The actual date, or even the year of the founding of the Portuguese Colony by Vasco da Gama is unknown to-day, but Robert Morrison refers to the year 1535. The Chinese official records admit foreign residence in 1550, but the Portuguese point to the year 1557 as the date of the colony's establishment.

The Emperor of China, grateful to the Portuguese for their ruthless but effective methods of handling the pirates and other brigands who infested the China coast even at that early date, granted them a narrow strip of land, where they reared up their stronghold and emporium, which they have succeeded in holding to this day. It was not until 1887, however, that China ratified by treaty the permanent occupation by the Portuguese of the colony and the adjacent islands of Veiue, Taipa and Colonane.

High up on this pointed promontory, at the confluence of the Pearl and West Rivers, on a high rock in the middle of the settlement is perched the old fort with its grim, grey walls and ancient cannons. At the foot of the rock stand the ruins of the ancient church of St. Paul, erected in 1565–1602, and built by the

Portuguese with the aid of Japanese Roman Catholic
converts who had been exiled from their country and
conveyed to Macao for safety. An imposing flight of
steps leads to the ruins, and in keeping with the romantic
and adventurous spirit of Macao, there are numerous
tales of treasure hidden in vaults beneath those steps.

There are about half a dozen hills on the peninsula,
all surmounted by forts, churches and monasteries. Here
also is the Guia, the oldest lighthouse on the China
coast.

To step ashore in Macao was to me like turning a
page of one of Stevenson's adventure tales. It is a
strange city, half Chinese and half Portuguese. Getting
acquainted with her was like learning to know one of
these half-caste Latin ladies.

She is angelic, beautiful and good when she is good,
but she is thoroughly bad when she is bad. She gambles,
reeks of opium fumes, and encourages all the other
sins usually thrown in with a thoroughly bad life. On
the other hand, she smiles at you innocently, lovely as
a church-going maiden on an Easter morning, and you
can accept her as such without being too much deceived.
However, you are the person who chooses her moods.
If you want her good, she is good ; if you want her
bad, she will certainly oblige you.

The outer appearance of this oldest European colony
in China is charming indeed.

Hidden away in a bay, surrounded by mighty green
hills, with long rows of pink, blue, or yellowish houses
along the water front, Macao reminds one of a piece of
picturesque Latin-American unexpectedly dropped down
and forgotten among China's hilly shores ; and the
presence of thousands of fishing junks and myriads of

sampans seems at first totally illogical in these European surroundings. Macao's industries, chiefly concerned with the production of preserved fish, fire-crackers, wine, and incense sticks, are of no great importance to the civilized world.

Macao practically ceased to play an important part in the occidental-oriental trade with the founding of Hong-Kong in 1841, only forty odd miles east of Macao. This British colony offers to the trade a more ample protection, both in harbour facilities and political prestige, than does Macao, and few ships find their way to the Portuguese colony nowadays.

The whole atmosphere of Macao is mediæval. It is a city of marked contrasts, "where the picturesque quaintness of a vanishing age is mingled with the enterprise of modern times." But one cannot get away from the feeling that this charming spot is dozing—with small chance of ever awakening.

Described by the tourist agencies as the "Gem of the Orient Earth," and as the Monte Carlo of the Far East, it richly deserves the first name, but there is very little justification for the latter. It lacks the tone, if not the spirit, of the palatial Casino of the French Riviera. As a matter of fact, there is no casino in Macao, but there are twelve dingy opium-reeking dives, the patrons of which wear no formal dress as is the rule at Monte Carlo. On a warm summer day you may rub elbows with half-naked coolies, road-dusty farmers, and fugitive embezzlers as you lay your bets on the gaming tables of Macao.

It is not far from the truth to say that the gambling passion rules the people of Macao. There is some kind of gambling going on all the time, whether it be *fan-tan*,

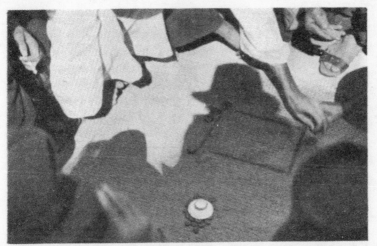

In the street corners fan-tan is played with beans

Macao lottery ticket shop

Interior of a Macao gambling house

played with beans or buttons on the pavement, lotteries, or merely dice. It is impossible to stroll casually down any street of Macao without seeing one or more groups of men, women and even children crowding around *fan-tan* mats or watching the "bones" turn up aces and sixes.

There are games played in every temple yard, next to the kowtowing, praying, fisherman's wife, or at the foot of the smouldering incense burner. I have seen decrepit old women fervently pray to the image of A-Ma, the patroness of the Chinese seamen, possibly for the safe return of beloved sons, or perhaps for the repose of departed souls, and at the next moment be in the middle of a spirited *fan-tan* game, in the shadow of another idol, black-bearded and ugly.

Perhaps even more universal than the other methods of gambling are the lotteries, of which three are held every day in Macao. At noon, at half-past seven in the evening, and at eleven in the evening Macao takes time off to learn the results of the draw. Everyone has a ticket, even if it is only for a cent or two, and all business stops while the results are announced.

You hear, of course, many stories of large winnings, but most of them are circulated by the brokers who sell the lottery tickets. I heard of one coolie who won $25,000, and subsequently drank himself to death—an enviable end for a Chinese rickshaw puller. I have also been shown mansions, surrounded by gardens and beautiful artificial lakes, said to belong to gentlemen whom Dame Fortune favoured in the draw.

Most of the ticket purchasers who have been in Macao long enough to acquire the habit watch eagerly for the results of each lottery, only to tear up their tickets after the draw and mutter the gambler's motto : " Better luck next time ! "

There are three different lotteries in Macao. First there is the *Pac Cap Pio*, with drawings three times a day. It is the poor man's lottery. It is for the rickshaw coolie, the street vendor, the urchin, the *sampan* hand, or anyone who wishes to risk a copper coin on the chance of making a hundred, perhaps a thousand per cent. on his capital.

Then there is the *San Pio*, with drawings once a week, the tickets of which are somewhat dearer, costing fifteen cents each. The same syndicate also handles another lottery with monthly drawings, the tickets of which cost forty cents, but with winnings correspondingly larger.

The *Po Pio* is the rich man's game. The ticket may cost anywhere from fifty cents to ten dollars (Chinese currency). The drawings are on every fifth day, and the street outside the *Po Pio* headquarters is crowded with a buzzing, expectant, excited throng of Chinese drawn from all classes and ages, both men and women.

During my occasional visits to Macao I bought one or more tickets daily, and once I actually received my purchase money back. But I never won.

Better luck next time !

The price of each ticket in the *Pac Cap Pio* lottery is one cent Chinese money, which is less than one half a cent United States currency. For ten cents the purchaser obtains ten or twelve tickets every day. Taking the brush from the shop-keeper's desk, he makes his ten marks on the tickets, selecting his characters at random from the eighty to choose from. Then one day—lo ! and behold ! six of these are winners. He is now so excited that he babbles

that next time he is most certainly going to win hundreds
—nay, thousands of dollars.   Next time !

The chief drawing of the *Pac Cap Pio* lottery takes
place at 7.30 p.m. The syndicate owns a large building on
one of the principal streets. The twenty lucky characters
are drawn in the presence of the public in a large room
on the ground floor. Outside, the street is blocked by
a crowd of coolies, messengers from the vendors, or
ticket-holders who mumble prayers to their special deities
to send them luck ; the dope fiend, for a few moments'
escape from his misery ; the dainty prostitute, for
regained freedom from a life into which she has been
sold by her *fan-tan* crazed parents ; the coolie, for money
to buy an extra bowl of rice.

There are two spherical copper containers in the rear
of the room. One contains eighty wooden balls, each
inscribed with a character corresponding to one of those
on the ticket. The other contains twenty red — the
winners, and sixty white balls—the losers. Four dirty-
looking attendants (one is cross-eyed and another minus
a nose) now start these copper containers rotating. The
wooden balls rattle noisily inside. Suddenly there is
silence. Two balls are simultaneously released, one from
each container, and another attendant picks up the one
with the lucky character, and in a sing-song voice
announces its name. Still another assistant picks up the
red or white ball and sings out the colour. Should
there be a character plus a white ball then this character
is a loser, but a character plus a red ball is a winner,
and a wooden disk carrying this character is hung high
on the wall. The coolies, the messengers, and the
prostitutes look eagerly at their tickets. And then
they turn away dejectedly, and walk slowly to the

nearest shop to buy another ticket.   Better luck next time !

*   *   *   *   *

The Macao Government derives a huge income from the monopoly granted to the *fan-tan* syndicate.   How many hundreds of thousands of dollars are paid yearly it is impossible to say with certainty.   In some of the houses the amount is given as $600,000, while at the house next door one is told that the syndicate pays over a million dollars.   Once I was given the figure of $1,800,000 or $5,000 per day, but I have reasons to believe that the actual figure looms somewhere just above $1,000,000.

Now, lest the reader accuse me of inexcusable slackness in not stepping up to the Government treasurer and asking for the official figures on the subject, I hasten to add that if one were foolish enough to do so one would most probably be requested to board the first steamer for Canton or Hong-Kong, and never to return.   Macao does not like anyone to pry into the details of her sinful life, and journalists are far from being beloved there.

The steamers, tourist-laden during the travel season, are always met by the hotel runners, the unavoidable coolies and the master-let-me-show-you-the-town-men. There are types like Opium Charlie, and Fan-Tan John —both Chinese—and then there are the half-castes, such as the Loafer and Harry the Dope.   They prey upon the tourists and faithfully show them the " secrets " of Macao, finally extracting a fee of one or two dollars. With this newly-acquired capital they depart hurriedly to the nearest *fan-tan* den, only to lose every cent of it. The Chinese must gamble to the last cent in his money belt, and when he has done so Charlie or John or Harry will come up to you and beg for a dollar, or failing to obtain that, for your small change.

Take the case of Opium Charlie. He has two wives, and his plea to me was the same every evening :

" Master, give me a dollar. Must buy food for wives."

" Master " had every reason to suspect that, at this rate, during his stay in Macao he was the chief support of Charlie's harem.

Charlie has been in Macao fourteen years, and has been seen at the *fan-tan* tables practically every night of that time. He says that he knows all about the game, and that the way you place your bet is simply foolish.

" Well, Charlie, you must be a rich man by now if you know all about this game."

To which Charlie does not reply, pretending not to have heard the remark.

He is an inveterate opium smoker—hence his nickname —and the money I gave him every evening was more likely smoked up than actually converted into cheap fish for the wives. He makes no secret of the fact that he loves his opium pipe. On the contrary, he believes himself to be something of a he-man, for all the world like a youngster who has been making secret use of his dad's briar. But when you see Charlie, and note his twitching features, his jumpy restlessness, and his parchment skin, you realize what havoc this beastly habit can play with a human body, mind, and nerves.

It is hard to believe Macao's protestations that she does not encourage the habit, since opium manufacturing and the sale of the refined product is by far the largest source of income to the Government of the colony.

Although the sum of over $200,000 collected annually

F

on the opium traffic alone is a small figure compared with
that of a few years ago, when the revenue exceeded
$6,000,000, the drug is sold freely, and there are, of course,
hundreds of wide-open opium-smoking dens in Macao.
Besides, opium is served as an ordinary refreshment in
the *fan-tan* houses, should the patron prefer a pipe to a
bottle of lemonade.   On the bill of fare it is quoted at
forty cents per smoke.

If at any hour of the night you pass through the
streets of Macao you will see numerous lighted lamps
suspended above the street corners advertising that
Sun Tai's or the Young Chung First Class Gambling
Company is located in the vicinity. If you hail a rickshaw
the coolie will pull you up to the door of the nearest
fan-tan den.   It is a foregone conclusion that every
foreigner is a gambler, and that the only places he is
expected to go to in Macao are these First Class Gambling
Companies.

A pair of turban-clad Indian policemen loiter in each
doorway, and the neighbourhood does not inspire one
with confidence. So you enter one of the casinos of
this Oriental Monaco. At first you see only a crowd of
decidedly rough-looking Chinese, a long table surrounded
by gamblers, and the attendants or *fokis*.*

The casino is built in two or three floors.   The

---

* A few words about the *fan-tan* game.

At the end of the table sits the " croupier," a half-naked
Chinese. His business is to count the " cash," the most important
and fateful part of the game. *Cash* is the familiar old-fashioned
Chinese copper coin with a hole in the middle.

In front of the croupier is a small heap of this " cash " hidden
beneath a brass cover, so that it is impossible for the onlookers
or the gamblers to count it. Presently the *foki* lifts the cover
and begins extracting coins, four at a time. He does it with a

ground floor, where the actual " gamble operations " are
going on, is for the " common rabble " ; but if you are a
tourist or an *habitué*, you watch the procedure through
an opening in the second floor and place your bets
through this hole. There is a sturdy rail to lean against
and chairs for your comfort, and an attendant takes
your stake, puts the money into a basket and lowers it
to the *fokis* around the table, meantime droning his
instructions as to how the bet is to be placed. There is
seldom a mistake, nor have I noticed any short-changing
when the bets were paid.

Good Chinese paintings and embroideries adorn the
rough, unpapered, and rather dirty walls, and caged
birds hang in the windows and the wide-open doorways.

The atmosphere is wholly and peculiarly China's own.
One must accustom oneself to it. Take the stench of bad

long stick, not touching the coins with his hands, thus avoiding
suspicion of cheating.

It is up to the public to guess how many coins will be left
for the last inward draw—whether *one*, *two*, *three* or *four*. If
you have guessed correctly, then you are a winner. You can
then collect profits equivalent to three times your bet, but a
charge of ten per cent. for the house will always be deducted
from your gross earnings. To bet in this manner, on one number
only, is called *faan*.

There are two or three square metal plates on the table with
money piled all around them. Each side of the plates represents
a number. The side towards the croupier is *one*. Number *two*
is the adjacent side to the left. *Three* is opposite *one*, and *four*
is to the right of *one*. Your bet is placed on the table in full
view next to the number you favour. You can also bet that
either of two adjacent numbers will come up. In other words,
you believe that either *one* or *two*, *two* or *three*, *three* or *four*,
or *four* or *one* will come up. This is called *kwok*, and you will
see your money placed on the corners between the numbers upon
which you place your bets. When you play *kwok* the odds are even.

tobacco, add thereto the odour of opium smoked by a couple of Chinese gentlemen leisurely reclining on the couch in the background of the room, season this mixture with the sharp odours of Macao's famous fish, plus those of common humanity—Chinese at that—and if you can stand all this you have something to brag about.   An attendant brings candy and places it before you with a small plate of water-melon seeds.   Unconsciously you nibble at these seeds when the *foki* begins the fateful counting of the " cash."   Another attendant hands you a kind of chart full of crosses, zeros, II's and III's, showing the last ten or fifteen winnings, and if you feel inclined to be governed by these previous results, you are at liberty to place your bets accordingly.   You can follow any system you wish or make your bets at random ; it is all up to you.   If you wish to bet according to the chart,

Then there is *nim*, or *lim* as the word sounds to me. You make one number the winner and one neutral.   In other words, should the neutral number come up, your money will be returned to you, while your winning number would have paid you two to one, less of course the ten per cent. to the house.

Ching is another way of playing.   You back one number and make the two adjacent numbers neutral, losing only if the opposite number should be the winner.   Odds are even.   Those who play *fan-tan* for a living prefer *Ching* to any other combination.

I do not believe that there can be much cheating in the *fan-tan* game.   All operations are performed by the croupier in full view of the playing public, and he places his " cash " in front of him and covers it up *before* anybody is allowed to make a bet.   The public is allowed to bet as it pleases, but the stakes cannot exceed five hundred dollars on *faan*, seven hundred and fifty dollars on *nim*, or one thousand five hundred dollars on *kwok* or *ching*. In other words, the possible loss of the house is limited to one thousand five hundred dollars on each bet.

you will have to learn the meaning of the mysterious signs appearing on it.

The zero stands for I, II for 2, III for 3, and the cross for 4.

*   *   *   *   *

To the right of me sits a pair of Chinese. The man is garbed in a long and costly silk robe, and the young girl with bobbed hair, ear - rings, and a high-necked blue gown is either his wife or his concubine. They play excitedly, and are noisily happy when they win ; but they are bad losers. Their bets are high, seldom under fifty dollars, and they argue about the probability of a certain number showing up. Heaven help the poor man if he makes the wrong guess, especially if he has placed his bets contrary to the advice of the lady.

Then there is the Portuguese lady who has her own peculiar method of deciding how to bet the next time. She takes a handful of water-melon seeds, counts them in *fan-tan* fashion, and the result is her lucky number. She has lost four times in succession.

The dainty prostitutes (most of them are dainty), sometimes three or four together, try their luck and are as happy as children if they are winners ; but they stamp their little feet angrily if they lose. However, they are far better losers than the man and his spouse next to me.

*   *   *   *   *

Then I see a hand stretched across the table. I see a flash of gold and the sparkle of a diamond.

A ring is pawned to provide capital with which to continue the game, and I note that all the money is placed on *one faan*. The most dangerous way to gamble ! That man must be either desperate or a dare-devil.

The moment the *foki* reaches for the cover and starts to count the " cash " there is silence. Not a word is spoken. The men nearest the *foki* try to count the coins as they lie in the heap on the table, and cunning in this art, they announce the result long before the *foki* has extracted even half of the coins. They are seldom mistaken.

*   *   *   *   *

This every-day drama had caught my attention, and I had forgotten to place my own bet. I wanted the man to win. The rabble below had placed their bets, and the pair next to me were still quarrelling. The little prostitute had also placed all her money on *one faan*. Oh, how I wanted them both to win !

Four and four the *foki* counted. Every sweeping movement of his left hand made the heap smaller.

" Yat ! " yelled a coolie at the top of his voice.

The *foki* still counted and finally I saw a single coin alone on the table. Yat ! (the number one in Chinese vernacular). *One* had won !

I tried to steal a look at the face of the man who had pawned the ring. A lot of money was turned over to him. He ran through the mass of bills I saw in his shaking hands. He redeemed his ring with a happy smile and, wonder of wonders, calmly walked out of the house !

There was not one who did not turn in surprise and look after him as his stooping shoulders disappeared through the dark doorway into the street. He was a wise man, indeed !

You cannot gamble on credit, nor is your cheque good. But you can offer your jewellery as security for advances of money with which to gamble. There are no charges for these loans. The gambler who is too poor to possess any gold or valuable stones, but who has a shirt or a pair of boots to pledge, can resort to any of the three or four pawnshops around the corner. They do a thriving business twenty-four hours a day.

Many are the pitiful stories about daughters sold as prostitutes to the brothels of Macao to provide their parents with means to satisfy temporarily their insatiable gambling passion.

One seldom hears of anyone trying to rob or hold up these gambling hells. For an enterprising Chicago gunman they would probably prove veritable paradises. The Chinaman is not built that way ; he would not dare do anything single-handed. He must have a mass behind him and with him. Then he is both brave and reckless, a robber and a murderer, and, according to home papers, he seems to prefer missionaries. Still the neighbouring islands are infested with pirates of the most dangerous type, and some of the peaceful green hills you can see from Macao's beautiful *praya's* are strongholds swarming with murderous banditti. Macao has no jurisdiction over these hills, nor these islands or their villages ; they belong to China Proper. Suppose that a group of enterprising gentlemen should decide upon a raid on the gambling dens of Macao and succeed ; there would be little use to register any complaint with the Chinese authorities. They would not have time to bother with bandits or pirates, for their countless civil wars require all of their attention. One almost suspects the existence of a " working agreement " between the gambling syndicate and the freebooters. Many of these are undoubtedly among the best customers of the gambling-houses ; indeed, one probably rubs elbows with them constantly as one leans against the barrier of the second floor of the " hell."

Many of the gamblers have no other home than these dens. Many are employed by the syndicate as guards against pickpockets. The streets are full of police, both uniformed and plain-clothes men, but it is seldom that a police whistle is heard within the gambling district of Macao.

PART THREE

" THIS CHINAMAN " came panting up the steps of the
Sun Tai *fan-tan* den, sat down beside me, and began
slowly to nibble at a handful of water-melon seeds. My
bet was one dollar on number *four*, but number *two* came
up and I lost the money.

Opposite me a giant Chinaman sat gambling heavily
—not one or two dollars, but fifty, a hundred, or two
hundred dollars at a time. And he won practically every
bet.

" Why don't you play with him ? " asked " this
Chinaman."

" What do you mean, ' play with him ' ? "

" Makee same bet as he makee."

And so I watched the man as he gambled. Very
soon he noticed my interest and smiled approvingly. He
appreciated the compliment I paid him by imitating him.
Any artist appreciates imitation as a compliment ; and
this man certainly knew the art of gambling at *fan-tan*.

Having won a sizable pile, the man retired to an
opium couch in the background of the room. A *foki* lit
the lamp.

" See that man ? " asked " this Chinaman," pointing
his thumb discreetly in the direction of the half-slumbering
opium-smoking giant.

" Who is he ? "

" Oh, vellee, vellee rich man. He find plentee gold,
old gold, Spanish gold, many years ago."

" Where ? "

" Oh, far away in Kaulan somewhere. Ship sink many years ago belong Poltuguese. Plentee gold. He coolie before, now vellee, vellee rich."

" How rich ? "

" No savee—ten thousand, ten ten thousand, hundred ten thousand." Meaning, 10,000, 100,000 and 1,000,000 as Chinese count.

" He speaks English ? "

" Hong-Kong coolie English."

So I sat down beside the man on the couch, greeted him in my best pidgin-English, and presently asked him to tell me about himself.

It is not polite to disturb a man when he is smoking opium. It is simply not done ; it is contrary to every rule of Chinese etiquette. But I, being a " foreign devil," would be excused, I knew, because of my ignorance of " Chinese proper fashion."

The giant cocked one eye at me sleepily. Then he opened both eyes and smiled.

" Sit down. Have pipe."

It is also not " Chinese proper fashion " to refuse a pipe, and I again was guilty of a breach of etiquette. Then I hurled a question at him, perhaps in somewhat of a blunt manner. Had he found a treasure ship—where and how ?

He yawned with such an effect that the *fokis* were forced to yell louder in order to make themselves heard. Noise was submerged beneath that yawn.

" Bye'm bye will tell. Not now. Too tiled. You play *fan-tan* now. I come back bye'm bye. We go topside my house."

There was a promise ! Here I had a successful

treasure hunter, a Chinese of the old type with a queue under his hat, and long, red finger-nails ; a labourer who had become a gentleman ; a coolie who had not drunk himself to death, but who had been wise enough to invest his money ; a common sailor who had become one of the richest men in Macao.

He fell asleep, and his slumber lasted perhaps twenty minutes, while I lost dollar after dollar in foolish gambling, with one eye on the *fan-tan* table and the other on the opium divan.

*   *   *   *   *

Outside the gambling-house we hailed three rickshaws and climbed into them.

The pullers plunged into a side street, climbed steep alleys leading to the ruins of St. Paul's Cathedral, and passing them, disappeared among the many small houses on the other side of the hill. Here we stopped in front of a gate opening into a large garden. A caretaker in a Chinese uniform opened the wicket for us, and our host led the way through the garden, past a large pond, over carved stone bridges, until at last we came to a white painted stone house, almost hidden in a grove.

Then he bade us enter.

Exquisite hardwood furniture filled the room ; Chinese silk paintings hung on the walls ; and a great deal of Ming, Kuang Hsi, Chen Lung, and Tao Kuang porcelain adorned the tables and shelves. Artificial flowers made of jade and other precious stones were imbedded in some of the vases, and a magnificent Ming screen divided the room into two parts.

We were invited to sit down, and presently two servants appeared with tea and sweet cakes.

I shall try to tell his story substantially as the man

told it to me. However, for the sake of clearness, I shall
use modern English idiom instead of pidgin-English.

About thirty years ago Nim Tai Yeoung was, indeed,
a poor coolie. He had never known his father, and his
mother had sold him as a small child to the owner of a
fishing junk. For years he sailed along the coast. Later
he also learned well the ways of the Canton River. He
sailed on the high seas all the way from Macao to Shanghai,
and one day in Shanghai he managed to run away from
the junk. After that he became a carrier coolie, from
which time he dated the hardest years of his life.

He wandered up the Yangtze River, and many a
junk he helped to pull up-stream with ropes burning deep
into his shoulders. Somehow he became the owner of a
small junk. Later he sold this in Shanghai, and made
use of the profits to return to Canton.

All the coast from French Indo-China to Hong-Kong
and Macao is more or less a *terra incognita*. Bold
Portuguese in the time of Vasco da Gama and his
followers plyed the waters from Canton westward.
Many a heavily-laden merchantman had foundered.
Many had been pirated. Many treasure chests had gone
down with the ships, but some had been buried by the
crews on the islands that dot this coast.

Nim Tai Yeoung joined a crew of desperate freebooters, and on the shores of an island called Kau Lan,
not so many miles south-west of Macao, he found a
treasure trove—old chests actually filled with Spanish
coin. He showed me some of the pieces ; they were coins
bearing dates from 1685 to the first part of the nineteenth
century. One coin, marked 1809, proved that this
treasure had been buried scarcely more than a century
ago.

I asked him if he thought there were more buried treasures hidden among the islands, and he replied :—

" I am certain of it.   There is an island near the Chicken Neck Strait.   Old sayings point to a fight between a Dutch merchantman and a Portuguese boat.   Both ships ran aground during the fight, and Chinese pirates made short work of the crews.   However, they were unable to find any treasure, and it is supposed that the captains had hidden their chests of gold and jewellery before the pirates arrived.   I have had men go through every inch of this island," he confessed with a smile, " and I have found nothing.   If you go there and see men at work they will be my men.   They have been working for three years, and they will work for three more ; then I will give up, but not before."

" How much gold did you find in Kau Lan, and why didn't the Chinese or Portuguese Governments claim the treasure ? "

" Oh, I don't know how much.   Not so much, after all.   The Chinese—well—I did not ask their permission, and nobody has objected to my finding anything.   As to the Portuguese, they have nothing to say about what I find on Chinese soil."

" But how much did you find ? " I pressed.

" Plenty for me to make a start."   And he smiled such a smile as only a Chinese can smile.

*   *   *   *   *

And now I shall try to describe in my own words the tale of the discovery.   It is a story worthy of a better pen than mine, and there is an intrigue in it which a dramatist might well adopt.   It is a love story.

It is not " Chinese proper fashion " to speak about

love, but Nim Tai Yeoung admitted that he had fallen in love with a young girl of much higher social rank than he—a simple coolie. But then, he wasn't exactly a coolie, either ; he was a junk-hand. The owner of the craft used to take his daughter along.

Nim was a young man, and sometimes the sea was calm, and the moon was bright, and the usual story repeated itself. Still, it wasn't the " Chinese proper fashion " to speak about love to the girl, and he kept the story of his passion to himself. So the girl spoke to him one night as they rowed ashore from the junk.

" You, Nim Tai Yeoung, are poor. My father is very rich, and I am his only daughter ; so now I am going to tell you a secret. On the island of Chicken Neck Strait and on the island south of that my father knows where gold is buried. I shall find out for you where it is. You will then be rich, and you can take me home with you."

But they did not kiss, nor speak foolish words, nor dream castles in the air, for such is not " Chinese proper fashion."

Since the time of Eden the woman has been the cunning one, ever leading the male into doing what he does not want to do. So it happened that the old man babbled to his beloved daughter the secret of the treasure trove. He had found it himself, and was going to lift it at the very first opportunity.

Nim Tai Yeoung gathered a crew of the toughest men he could get ; there was many a murderer wanted by the law, many a thief, and many a pirate among them. They were all glad to join him in his quest for gold.

He never told me how he got the junk in which they sailed.

When the father discovered that his daughter had

eloped with the ne'er-do-well junk-hand, he hoisted sail and started in pursuit. Instead of sailing west the elopers had sailed east, and in the darkness of the night they doubled back on their course, thus fooling the old man and reaching the shore.

Now it must be told that the only arms on board the ship were two pistols—ancient muzzle-loaders carried by Nim Tai Yeoung. At sunrise the next morning he gathered his crew together, and his wife brought a white rooster to be slaughtered ; then the men swore allegiance to the new chief, promising that if any gold was found one-third should be divided among the men while Nim Tai Yeoung and his bride should retain the other two-thirds for themselves.

The treasure was found, the young woman leading the way, and that was the beginning of Nim Tai Yeoung's fortune.

For five years he sailed on this and other junks. Through warfare or by peaceful negotiation he acquired a reputation as a freebooter and " protector." Finally, he retired.

Such was Nim Tai Yeoung's simple tale of treasure trove, of piracy, of love, and of a desperate bandit crew under the glistening sails of a pirate junk.

*　　　*　　　*　　　*　　　*

" Nim," I asked, " between ourselves, are you still a pirate ? "

He smiled the usual Oriental smile. He clapped his hands as a signal for the servants to bring more tea and sweets, and then he answered my question.

" I only gamble now and then, but somehow I *always* win." He stressed the word " always."

An idea struck me that in some way he probably was doing a " protecting " business in the *fan-tan* houses ; but he only smiled and offered me more tea.

I then asked him if he intended going on any more treasure hunts. He looked at me quizzically and said : " Would you care to go with me ? "

" Would you take me ? "

" I believe that I would ; but if bad men come against me, would you fight with me ? "

I replied that I most certainly would—in fact, that I should love it.

And so he promised to send a messenger to Hong-Kong when he was ready to make another trip.

PART FOUR

GORDON MCCLINTOCK was a soldier. He had joined the
Royal Forces between the sixth and seventh glass of
whisky while in a desperate mood, having been turned
down by his "sweetie," and finding that his finances
consisted of one shilling and sixpence. Forthwith he was
sent to Hong-Kong, and after three months decided to
escape because he did not like the army life.

But Gordon McClintock was caught five yards outside
the barrack limits, and duly received fourteen days in
the guard-house, a fact which did not by any means
increase his love for the army.

His next attempt had been to get himself discharged
from the Service. He had talked the matter over with
the patrolman directing the traffic on the corner of
Queen's Road and Ice House Street in Hong-Kong. So
Gordon arranged with the police officer to be arrested,
and at the first opportunity which presented itself, our
brave soldier strolled into a jewellery store, "pinched" a
ten-dollar watch, and walked up to the patrolman,
shouting: "Hey! I made it! Here is the watch!
Put me in!" Whereupon they marched to the police
station, and Gordon McClintock was sentenced to three
months' hard labour for petty larceny.

But he did not secure a discharge from the army!

*   *   *   *   *

I met Gordon McClintock in a bar in Kowloon, a

suburb across the straits from Hong-Kong proper, where, full of beer and disappointment, he told me the story of his prison experience. It was not a pleasant tale.

He told of white officers kicking Chinese prisoners at the slightest provocation ; of white prisoners being forced to walk over the gallows platform when they were taken out for daily exercise ; of early morning hangings just outside the white prisoners' cells ; of terrible food ; and of cockroaches and centipedes crawling about the cells at night ; of floggings and screaming prisoners ; and of convicts who went mad when forced to walk day after day, week after week, and month after month, in a narrow circle, lifting to their waists at every third step a heavy iron cannon-ball.

" Tell me, McClintock, are there many pirates in prison now ? "

After ordering another glass of beer, he said : " There sure are, but if the officials found out that they were pirates they would be hanged. Pirates are always hanged."

And through that night and many more nights I thought over what this soldier had told me. Behind the grey walls of Victoria Jail there were perhaps tales to fill a book, and one foggy morning after a sleepless night I wrote a letter. The letter was addressed to my editor, the man who had sent me on the quest for pirates. I asked for permission to go to prison.

Twenty-nine days later I received the following cablegram :

" Would like very much to see a story as you suggested in your letter. . . .

" (Signed)."

I went to consult a solicitor; upon learning what I wanted to do he threw me out—not bodily, but with a haughty gesture. However, he offered magnanimously to take over my defence if I should need one, but he would not be an instrument whereby the dignity of a Court of Justice should be ridiculed. He refused to give me any advice as to the best means of getting into trouble, and consequently into jail. So I went to another solicitor.

I had bad luck there, too, but he also offered his services as a defence lawyer in case of need.

The third was a good old Scotchman. He had a grudge against the Government, and was enthusiastic about disclosing all the "dirt" about the "walled city" within Hong-Kong, and he gave me some good advice. I am not sure he was a Scotchman, either, for he did not charge me a cent for the advice; on the contrary, he offered to aid me to get into trouble.

*   *   *   *   *

I was arrested and remanded to a cell in the Victoria Jail, examined, re-examined, and again examined, and when the judge boomed, "Two months!" I must admit that I did not feel well.

The lawyer whom the Scotchman had advised me to employ as my defence counsel did his best to get me out, but he became exasperated when I made things look so bad for myself that in the end I could almost have been committed for murder.

The Crown's advocate asked me if I had any connection with the pirates, to which I had replied, "I refuse to answer."

"Did you receive a messenger from a notorious Macao brigand on such and such a night?"

This was the messenger Nim Tai Yeoung had sent to me when he was ready to go on the treasure hunt in which he had invited me to participate. As long as his name was not mentioned, I did not see why I should refuse to answer the prosecuting attorney.

"Yes, I did!"

"What was the message?"

I refused to answer.

"Who was the man who sent the messenger?"

I refused to answer.

So I became a convict.

I was duly finger-printed, measured, weighed and given a number, E-10121. I was vaccinated by an Indian hospital guard with hands that were none too clean. Later they made me undress, and a severe-looking hospital doctor pounded me on the chest. Then I was told to dress; they locked me into the cell five feet by seven in size, where I had been kept for several weeks as a remand prisoner.

The furniture consisted of a wooden board attached to the wall—it served as a table. There was a shelf higher up in one corner of the room and a somewhat larger one near the floor in the opposite corner. A metal cup full of drinking water and a wash-basin occupied the larger shelf. A cuspidor stood in one corner of the room, and in the corner next to the door was another basin with a cover. That was the w.c., but the "w" was missing. The walls of the room were white-washed. Near the ceiling there was a small window, barred, of course, but fortunately I was permitted one electric lamp. The bed consisted of a straw mattress, with sheets, a hard pillow and two woollen blankets, all marked with the well-known arrow and the letter " E," which meant " European."

Being accustomed to hardships, I decided to make the best of it, but at the same time I could not help believing myself to be the biggest fool on earth. However, I hoped some good " copy" might come of my experience.

I was brought from court some time after five o'clock in the afternoon. The jails closed officially at six. A cup of mush was thrust under my cell door, together with a piece of bread. This was the evening meal. I could hear a cell nearby being locked and unlocked, and then my door was opened with rasping keys.

" Getcher water for the night ! Hurry up ! "

I filled the cups with water in the hall corridor and shuffled back to the cell. The door was banged behind me and locked. It sounded as if there were two different locks. I was secure inside for the night. The light was turned on at six o'clock and left burning until eight.

As soon as the warder of " D " hall had left for the night, after having counted all of the prisoners and reporting the number to the principal warder, and after the total number of prisoners had been found to be correct, pandemonium broke loose. All the " boarders " of " D " hall began a lusty chorus of singing and shouting, and as most of the singers were Chinese, the din was terrible. One individual went on in an almost endless melody pitched in a high falsetto voice, and after the first week I would have gladly assisted in hanging him, had a chance been offered.

Then there were the cockroaches ! They came from under the door—big, black and fat, three inches or more in length. I thought they were mice, and chased them all around the cell until I bumped into the wall and began cursing with such an effect that the night guard looked through the hole in the door and asked, " Whattsa matter ? "

" Give me some light ; I have mice here."

All my hall mates heard me, and pandemonium reigned again. All of them had gone through the same experience.

As a remand prisoner, I had been allowed to receive letters and do some writing. I had had ample time to keep a diary, for I was not allowed to do any labour, having been locked in and practically kept in solitary confinement during the weeks before the judge had his final say.

A remand prisoner is not really considered a prisoner, yet he is submitted to harsher treatment than a convict. There is something wrong with the system, and it certainly does not put the prisoner in a frame of mind to fight the police, the Crown attorneys, and the accusers.

The prison food was not fit to be eaten by a European. It consisted for the most part of starch—potatoes, wheat flour mixed with mutton fat, oatmeal mush, and bread. Then there was a soup so hot with pepper that it fairly blistered my mouth. During my sojourn in the Victoria Jail, I ate soup five times ; three times out of the five I managed to keep it down.

Twice a week we received two slices of meat boiled in a very fat and highly-spiced liquor. As we had no knives or forks (prison " silverware " is limited to spoons), I had to tear the meat to pieces with my fingers, and a hard job it was.

Anyone who has ever owned a dog knows how the food

is usually served to him—in a metal pannikin. In such a manner was our food served to us in Victoria Jail.

We were not allowed to shave, but were permitted to use the common clippers. There were two pairs of clippers in the prison—one for the Europeans and another for the Chinese. They probably never had been disinfected, a fact which meant that one stood every chance of infection, because prisoners afflicted with leprosy, syphilis, and other contagious diseases had access to the clippers in the same way as anyone else.

I have seen Chinese prisoners submitted to downright cruelty by the white and Indian warders and guards ; kicking, beating, and slapping were everyday occurrences. Chinese prisoners were seldom addressed but with a very foul word which, although it is Chinese, I cannot repeat.

I must admit, however, that the guards were decent enough to the few European prisoners who were "boarding" at this Government hotel.

*   *   *   *   *

On my first night in prison, just after I had been brought in from the court as a remand and locked in a cell, I was confidentially told by the Indian guard : "Chinee man hang to-morrow."

"Where ? "

"Outside, right outside here."

And he pointed to the cell opposite mine. The gallows were in the narrow courtyard a few yards to the right of the cell window.

That night all the prisoners on the gallows side of the hall were removed to another building. The doors of the cells were left open.

I lay awake half the night trying to work out a plan for getting in touch with the Chinese pirates whom

the Earless One had named.   On the face of it it seemed
impossible to communicate with anybody inside the
" dead city."   Communication between prisoners was
absolutely forbidden.

Still, there might be a way.

Perhaps I had been a fool after all.   What of it ?   A
few weeks, and this adventure would be ended.

*   *   *   *   *

I awoke early.   It could not have been later then five,
for I could see the stars twinkling through the narrow
window.   Somewhere out in the darkness I could hear
shuffling feet.

Somebody asked in a muffled voice :

" Everything all right ? "

" Yes, everything's all right."

" Bring him out."

More shuffling of feet.   Silence.

Then the crash !

My heart beat wildly.   I crept up to the door and
tried to look through the peep-hole.   There was a shadow
on the opposite cell wall, and through the bars of the
window I could see a strong lamp burning outside.   In
its light there was a second dark shadow swaying slowly
—back and forth, back and forth.

Another muffled voice.

" I think he is gone."

" Not yet ! "

" Well, let him hang fifteen minutes."

When a quarter of an hour had passed I saw the
shadow of a hand cut down the rope ; then the dark
object dropped out of sight.   That was the end of my
first night !

At seven in the morning the other European prisoners were allowed to come back to their quarters. Being a "remand," I wore my own clothes. The others were dressed in prison garb with arrows and numbers—black arrows for short sentences and red arrows for long ones. A short sentence man is any prisoner "doing time" for less than two years.

At nine in the morning they led me out to the exercise yard. A guard took me to the second floor of "D" hall, and from there we walked over a concrete bridge into a narrow yard! There was a hole in the middle of the bridge and the guard warned me to be careful. Then, half-turning, he said : "This is the gallows."

Involuntarily I shuddered. I felt as though I had touched a warm body, newly dead.

After a short march through another hall we reached the exercise grounds. Several hundred Chinese were grouped in one part of the yard doing "hard labour." At first I thought it was a joke when the guard whispered : "This is the hard labour of this jail." They were all squatting in rows, with piles of hemp rope stubs heaped in front of them. All day long the prisoners sit there unravelling this hemp, often with bleeding fingers, making caulking material for use in the navy. In the middle of the yard was a group of men who were doomed to walk in a circle month after month—the "stone and the shot" men. One group carries the stones and another the shots, and all the time they walk in a circle. Occasionally somebody breaks out in a high-pitched laughter mingled with screams. A maniac !

Seven European prisoners were walking in the exercise yard. The exercise consists in marching round in a large circle in single file, each man stepping in the tracks of the prisoner in front of him. I wanted to join them, and slip them a word of greeting.

But as I moved toward them a short, cocky, under-sized guard—a European at that—stepped up to me, pushed me in the back with a sharp command: "You can't mix with the prisoners. You are a remand. This way! Hurry up!"

That man must have been an M.P. some time in his life. He was the only one I really learned to hate in Victoria Jail.

*   *   *   *   *

But what about my pirates?

How could I get in touch with any of them? While walking about for half an hour I brooded over this problem without seeing any possible solution.

Sometimes as I sat in my cell I could hear horrible screams as from a man being tortured or slowly murdered. Then a sickening swish. Then again swish, swish! And every time the screams would grow less intense.

That was flogging!

And then, when I was sentenced to two months' "hard labour," I was cut off from the world; I was not allowed to read or write any letters, nor to receive any from the outside—at least, not until it had been censored by the prison authorities. I had no idea whether or not the Press had followed my "case"; still, I had every reason to believe it had, and I thought of my friend, Chang Liu, who must have heard of my success in getting into the Victoria Jail. I wondered if he had enough sporting blood in his veins to contrive to send me a message, and perhaps to suggest a means of com-municating with his friends. He had never admitted that he knew anything about the pirates. The Earless One had babbled all that information. And the Earless One might have sent me to the jail as a Chinese joke! Many a time I thought that my adventure had been a grand failure.

*   *   *   *   *

There had been new Chinese remand prisoners received in " D " hall.

As a matter of fact, there were remand prisoners arriving every day, but somehow this noisy crowd drew my attention more than any other. As I lay in my bed trying to read a silly book in the dim light that came in through the window a paper was thrust under the door. I thought it was only the daily ration of three sheets of toilet paper, and continued to read. A quarter of an hour later I reached for the paper, and to my astonishment I found three groups of figures written on it. What the —— ?

Three—there was no mistake about it. Here was a message to me, but what did those figures mean ? Was it a code ? I studied it diligently, and could make nothing of it. Then I decided that the whole thing must have been a mistake. It must have been that one of the guards had written down some of the numbers of the newly-arrived prisoners on the first bit of paper he got hold of. That must surely be the explanation, I thought.

And so I put away the paper on the shelf and continued to read the book.

There were shuffling footsteps outside my cell. The guard was making his rounds. I could feel him looking into my cell ; then I heard him shuffle away.

There was another paper on my floor !

Did they expect an epidemic of diarrhœa ? Such a luxury of extra toilet paper ! Then I saw three groups of figures written on this ration—exactly the same as before. So this *was* a message after all ! Suddenly it dawned on me that these figures must be the numbers of certain prisoners.

Who could have sent the message ? It must have been given to the guard either by a new remand prisoner or by a Chinese from outside. I memorized the three numbers and then destroyed the papers. There was a heavy penalty for receiving uncensored messages from outside the prison. Guards who smuggle anything to the prisoners are liable to receive two years' imprisonment.

I remembered those numbers well. I intended to make every effort to discover those three Chinese among the prisoners, but how to get a chance to speak with them ! Who could have sent the message ? I pondered over that question for hours. There were only two persons who knew my actual motive for going to jail. I decided it could only have been Chang Liu ; for after all, the Earless One was most likely only Chang Liu's man. There was no doubt that all of our conversation had been reported to Chang Liu—it must have been so. And now Chang Liu had taken the trouble and risk of sending a cryptic message that I could barely understand.

*   *   *   *   *

The next morning at eleven o'clock the guard came for me, and again we walked over the gallows to the exercise yard. At one end of the yard a camera was propped up on a tripod and operated by a Chinese. One

European guard watched over a large number of Chinese who squatted round him. One of them was marking in a book the number of prisoners and the number of pictures that were required of each. Another was busy putting together block numbers, and a third one was writing Chinese characters in chalk on a small blackboard. Both the block numbers and the blackboard were attached to the prisoner's coat when he posed before the camera.

I happened to glance at each man's prison number.

Luck was with me! There was one of the numbers that had puzzled me in yesterday's message. It adorned the coat of a young Chinese whose red arrows indicated that he was a long-term prisoner, *i.e.* in jail for more than two years.

Finally it came to my turn to be photographed! The man with the red arrows handed me a dark blue serge coat to put on. As I slipped into the coat I half-turned to him and whispered:

"I want to talk to you. Chang Liu has sent me."

Have you ever seen a Chinese turn pale? This one did more, he actually turned green. At first a startled look came into his eye, and then I read terror. His arms dropped to his sides, and he stammered:

"You-you talkie Chan-Chang Liu?"

A harsh voice barked out:

"Hey, you, stop talking!" and a guard came striding towards us. My picture was snapped and I was led back to my cell, without any further opportunity to speak to Red Arrow.

Apparently I had guessed correctly. The message was from Chang Liu. I had to find a way to talk to these prisoners—but how?

One night I became suddenly ill with a fever, accompanied by symptoms of what I believed to be dysentery. It was after the hour when the lights went out, but I was too sick to care what happened to me. Once when the guard passed my door and let the light from his lamp play under the door while he peeped through the eye-hole I shouted to him that I was sick.

The attacks came so often and so suddenly that I must have lost consciousness, for the next thing I have recollection of was an Indian hospital warder and the principal warder, a European, standing over my cot. The Indian was taking my pulse.

" One hundred twenty," he said, " we will have to get him to the hospital."

That night I left my cell, never to see it again.

In the hospital I was shown a bed with a dirty sheet. An Indian lifer—a murderer—had been ousted from it. I remember saying to the hospital warder : " For goodness' sake, let me have a clean sheet at least."

" What do you think this is ?   The Peninsula Hotel ? You'll get it to-morrow ! "

I was too ill to protest.

I remained in the hospital the rest of my sentence— almost the entire two months.

The superintendent came in the next day. He was a likeable chap.

Approaching my bed, he said : " Well, what is the matter ?   Cholera or dysentery ?   You know, in this hotel they either die or get well."

I then complained about the dirty sheet, with the result that a clean one was on the bed within a few minutes. As soon as the superintendent was gone a doctor came and counted my pulse. At the same time the hospital warder took my temperature without wiping the thermometer, which had been used on the Chinese prisoners a few moments before.

The doctor was an amiable man. He asked me a thousand questions and supplied the answers himself. Then he told the warder to give me a few needles of something somewhere, and for a couple of days I was unable to sit. Still, those needles helped me a lot. While I was receiving the injections the superintendent came in again. As soon as we were alone I told him about the dirty thermometer.

" You know," he confided, " I am almost glad that you are here. I am going to ask you to tell me all about this hospital and its faults, but report these things only to me—not to the doctor or anyone else. The Chinese would never dare report anything that goes wrong, for they fear the warder will beat them up or give them an extra dose of castor oil."

That night bed-bugs almost devoured me.

Fritz, a German, with a huge birth-mark on his face, occupied the bed next to me ; he also had stomach trouble. He had been sentenced to two years' imprisonment for trying to sell a pistol to a Chinese while his ship was in harbour. Fritz was a good fellow ; we talked German together. He had not spoken a German word during the entire six months he had been in prison, and he actually wept tears of joy when he learned I could speak it. German was the only language he knew, and the few words of English he had acquired did not help him much.

The second cot from mine was occupied by a feeble-minded Scotch soldier. According to his story, he had been a sleep-walker, and had wakened in most peculiar places upon numerous occasions. One night he had wakened on top of a bus ; another night in a restaurant, sitting at a table and having a meal served to him. Of course, he had been unable to pay. On yet another occasion he had found himself in a jewellery store with his hands full of watches ; however, I have a suspicion he was not asleep that time. But he insisted that he was, and he had told the judge the same story.

But evidently the judge had not believed him.

On the last cot—there were four along the wall—was a Finn. He spoke only Finnish—poor chap. He had gone as a stowaway from Shanghai, had been caught, of course, and turned over to the police in Hong-Kong. The judge had sentenced him to three weeks' hard labour, or a $25 fine. As he had no money, he served the three weeks ; later he was going to be sent back to Shanghai. He too had stomach trouble.

On the opposite side of the room there were four Chinese, each of whom spoke a dialect which the others did not understand.

However, I understood one thing—they had been bitten by bed-bugs that night.

I told the hospital warder about it the first thing in the morning.

He laughed at me and said : " They have been here longer than you have."

When the hospital superintendent came in I repeated this answer to him. I shall not write what the hospital superintendent said, but he did say a good deal, and he ordered the hospital warders and the yard-boys— trusties—to wash the entire hospital with disinfectants. He asked me, *a prisoner*, to see to it that the Indian hospital warders did their job.

I was no favourite with the hospital warders after this.

*   *   *   *   *

At all hours during the day and night an Indian guard paced up and down the ward. I knew that he had been spitting on the floor, and one night I caught him in the act. What hospital hygiene !

I fairly flew at him. He told me to go back to my bed, and threatened to hit me with his night stick if I didn't get back quickly. I looked him over and obeyed— he was a husky chap. The next morning I reported this incident to the hospital warder. The guard told him that I was a liar, and that he had only told me to go back to bed when he had found me walking around the ward.

Fritz the Scotchman and the Finn all told me that I, a prisoner, was foolish to try to get justice in the face of a guard's testimony. This had never been achieved before.

The hospital warder reported me for disobedience to the guard, the penalty of which was ten days on bread and water. The superintendent came in looking very severe, and asked me what the rumpus was about. The guard was called in. He shook his head violently when I accused him of spitting on the floor ; then to my great surprise I received support from an entirely unexpected source. The four Chinese all started to babble at once —each one in his own dialect. Our combined testimony was enough to prove that the guard had a habit of spitting on the floor.

He changed his habits !

*   *   *   *   *

The bath tub in the adjacent bathroom was never used, at least not for bathing. The yard-boys came in

H

daily to fill it with water and wash out the cuspidors, and the Chinese prisoners used to brush their teeth in it. Finally I persuaded the superintendent to order this bath tub to be thoroughly cleaned, and to permit us to use it once a week for a bath. After he had considered the matter for a couple of days we had our baths.

The blankets on the hospital cots, as far as I could find out, had not been changed, aired, or disinfected for four months. They were dusty, dirty, and vermin-infested. I suggested to the superintendent that the bedding should be taken out and aired by the yard-boys, but I did not succeed in bringing this about.

Two months later, when I left the prison, the same blankets were still on my cot ; probably they will be for months to come.

*   *   *   *   *

At ten minutes to six in the morning a bell jangled a loud signal to wake up. At six o'clock two more bells announced breakfast. At seven there were again two bells—the call to work. Other bells rang at seven-thirty and eight-thirty and at nine o'clock. The first dinner bell rang at ten-thirty, followed by another at eleven-fifteen, when the work ended. When the guard went to dinner at eleven-fifty this fact was also advertised by two bells. Then there were hourly bell signals at one, two, three and four o'clock, when the prisoners quit working. At four-thirty the supper call was rung. A bell at five o'clock announced the roll-call, and the last one rang at five-thirty at the change of guards, when the night-watch came on duty.

*   *   *   *   *

In our ward was a Chinaman who spoke some kind of

strange dialect which nobody understood. He had been jailed four times during the last year. He came back within a week after being released on each occasion, each time for the same crime—cutting trees on Government property. He had a bad case of ringworm, and wished to be cured. As he could not afford the expensive injections, he had decided that to go to prison was a good way to get free treatment, and so he came back with astonishing regularity with his sentence doubled every time. The last time he had been sentenced the judge had said that he could not understand his passion for tree-cutting, but the good prison doctor understood. I even believe that he had been experimenting with new cures upon the man. Unfortunately, however, the Hong-Kong Government finally decided to get rid of this free patient, and a few days before he was released he was surprised to find that a deportation order was waiting for him.

Outside our ward was a separate cell for the criminally insane. There was one inmate who seemed to be harmless, and he was allowed to come into our ward to use the lavatory.

One night he was in a rather grousy mood. The grille door was opened with much clanking, and the man passed through. This chap was in for twenty years; he had been a highway robber, and everybody was convinced that his insanity was simulated. Sometimes he forgot that he was insane, and I understood that upon these occasions he talked interestingly, and sometimes was astonishingly clever, but this day he was very much out of humour. The Indian guard was instructed to keep an eye on him. The poor devil decided after much grumbling that he was going to take a bath, but he did not care to fill the tub with clean water. Instead, he emptied the cuspidors into the tub and climbed into it. The guard had been busy looking out of the window, which he should not have done, and all at once we heard a great splashing of water and much snorting; the boy was enjoying himself immensely.

The guard rushed into the bathroom, night-stick in hand. The next moment several cuspidors came flying into the ward, crashing into atoms. Then both men fell through the swinging half-doors. The prisoner was getting the best of the fight, so we Europeans decided to take a hand in it.

The scene was not very unlike a football team in practice. Then somebody touched the alarm bell, and all the European and Indian guards rushed in, armed with night-sticks and pistols.

There was a lot of reporting to be done, and the guards came in and took our testimony, because the matter would have to be reported to the prison superintendent the next day. The offender was removed from the prison to the hospital for the criminally insane.

And that was probably all he had wanted; he had finally succeeded in getting out of the worst prison in the British Empire.

*   *   *   *   *

A Chinese died in the next ward. He died of beriberi. There was a commotion, and the patients stretched their necks to see him pass out. We in the European ward could see him through the grilles which separated our ward from his. When it was over and someone had closed his eyes, it was suddenly discovered that there was a screen which was supposed to be put up in front of dying or dead patients. The screen was kept in the bathroom. Some of the guards were sent forthwith to fetch it, but when they touched it hundreds of cockroaches descended on the bathroom floor in a shower. Immediately there ensued a general and boisterous hunt for these well-fed vermin.

Later in the morning we could see the dead man stretched out on the stone bench in the morgue on the ground floor just within the entrance to the prison; from the hospital window one could see everything that happened within the morgue. The doctor cut him up, and the sight was rather gruesome. Yet we took it in with interest, because of the measure of relief from the monotony which even this scene brought us. Then a voice boomed through the grille. It was the chief warder, a Scotchman, a three-hundred pounder, with vicious walrus moustaches.

" Hie, you are supposed to be sick. Get down to your beds."

And so we went to bed for another month.

*   *   *   *   *

There was another occasion which never failed to bring us hustling around the window. The entrance to the women's prison was just under the window next to my bed. Two or three times a day the gate was unlocked and thirty or forty of these women convicts emerged through it, carrying garbage cans or fetching their food. Whenever the keys clanked in the gate all the inmates of our ward rushed to the window—European and Chinese alike. But I shall pass over the remarks they made and the criticisms offered, especially by the European prisoners.

The white prisoners clamoured for more food, because patients in the hospital ward get only half rations. In bad cases the doctor ordered some addition to the menu, such as milk and eggs. Because I could not eat my soup or the so-called pudding—wheat flour boiled with chopped-up pieces of mutton fat—I used to give my portion away to the other prisoners. This had to be done in secret, for if I had been detected it would have meant a sentence to bread and water. Sometimes when the guard's back was turned the potatoes flew from bed to bed like tennis balls. The Chinese also coveted the bread and potatoes. The food which they received was even worse than that of the European prisoners. Three times a day for seven days a week they ate brown rice and occasionally a small fish, salted or cooked. They drank ink-black tea, and as they ate they would squat on their beds and spit fishbones on the floor.

*   *   *   *   *

During the rest of my "sojourn" there were two more hangings.

A Chinese had butchered his partner with a meat cleaver. After chopping up his friend the murderer was at peace with the world, at least he said so while in the death cell and when he was brought to the gallows. He was glad to die, he shouted. The affair was carried off according to the usual procedure at five o'clock in the morning, while the stars were still shining brightly in the cloudless sky. There was the usual shuffling of feet, the crash of the trap, and a doctor's muffled decision that life had fled from the swinging body. We saw this man brought to the morgue; we saw the hangmen turn the limp body on its back and prepare it for burial.

Later in the day there was hammering in the yard below. The dead man was being put into his coffin.

A week later the other man was hanged with exactly the same procedure. Always half an hour before we expected the crash of the trap everyone was wide awake and waiting to hear it.

*   *   *   *   *

One day I was called to the prison superintendent's office. The chief warder himself brought me to him. I had already seen this official on several occasions, the first time having been when I received my official introduction to him upon being admitted to the prison.

There was a long row of Chinese prisoners waiting to see him too. And whenever an official passed them they lifted their hands, palms outward, showing that they carried no concealed weapons. Or perhaps it was a new way of saluting.

The superintendent was a retired major in the army, and he looked the part. He looked very much retired, indeed, and not too healthy. He was a small man, but very important.

" Ahem ! " he said when he saw me. " We are quite surprised in this prison," he said, " ahem, that you have been receiving large amounts of money from various parts of the world. How is this, and why ? "

I told him that several editors had kindly remembered to pay for stories of mine that they had published, and that it was likely I should get still more. Although my correspondence, readdressed by the United States Consulate to the Victoria Jail, was censored, and I was not allowed to receive a single letter, the bank matters had to be attended to, and certain receipts had to be signed. While the superintendent hemmed and hawed, I took a malicious pleasure in signing receipts for $1,500.

"Ahem," he said again, "I really don't understand why men like you should get into prison. After all, ahem! after all—ahem! well, that is all for to-day."

The three-hundred pounder barked :

"Stand at attention!" Then he boomed, "Dismissed!" And I shuffled off to my hospital cot.

That night shortly after nine o'clock the principal warder, a lesser prison official, came in. He sometimes entered our ward to get a drink of water, and occasionally he stopped at my cot and chatted for a few minutes.

"Say," he said, "what are you really doing in jail ? "

"Well, I think I am going to write it up."

"For heaven's sake don't mention any names! If you do, and especially if you tell of any of us warders or guards having been kind to you, we'll get the ' sack.' "

And after that, when he was on duty, he came in regularly, and I carefully led him into telling me more about the prison. And finally I found out that the third " number " with whom I wanted to get in touch had been recently released, but "was expected back shortly."

*   *   *   *   *

After all, I did not gain very much by my prison adventure, at least not in the way of information about pirates, but I believe that the experience was invaluable for future " copy." I finally gave up all hopes of communicating with the pirates in prison, and a few weeks before my release I began to plan my next activities. I had plenty of time to do it, only disturbed by the mess-calls and the hospital doctor's injection needle. This was the most distressing feature of my whole experience, because it hurt grievously, and it still hurts as I write this, four months later.

I had grown a beard, but the assistant chief warder ordered me to shave it off. Prisoners were not allowed to grow beards. There were three reasons why I did not want to shave it off: first, I refused to use the insanitary prison clippers; second, I had decided to go back to Macao, and if possible to get in touch with some of the pirate gangs opposed to Lai Choi San and her gang—the beard would be a very good disguise; third, I did not want my friends in Hong-Kong to recognize me on the streets, rush over to me, shake my hand violently and say, " I am so glad to see you out of prison! How was it in there ? "

There was a lot of fuss about my beard because I stubbornly refused to have it shaved off. The warder insisted that I should get rid of it, and so that matter went the whole way up to the superintendent, who was to decide finally whether or not I should be allowed to grow hair on my face. In fact, it seemed to have become a matter of precedence.

I was permitted to grow my beard.

*   *   *   *   *

At last I was released.

My mail was handed over to me, and the chief warder shook my hand and told me not to come back again.

I took a taxi to an hotel, where the manager met me with a smile and a greeting, and a curse upon his lips addressed to all the Government officials in Hong-Kong. He gave me the best room he had, and ordered a luncheon. And what a luncheon it was!

Then the assistant hangman walked in. We had luncheon together.

PART FIVE

THE following day I took a boat to Macao. I met an American on board, and he gave me all the news covering the last three months.

There had been a piracy toward the end of September. A Japanese ship, the *Delhi Maru*, had been pirated, and *at the head of the gang had been a woman!*

A woman! Could it have been Lai Choi San? It seemed impossible, because I knew that she did not approve of high-seas piracies of steamships. On the other hand, she had confessed to me on several occasions her hatred for the Japanese. I was suddenly filled with a desire to see the Pirate Queen and talk over the affair with her.

I soon found out that Madame Lai Choi San was not in Macao. Again I combed the gambling-houses and the opium dens and made numerous inquiries, but nobody seemed to know anything concerning her whereabouts. In Hong-Kong I had engaged a new interpreter and a servant, a pidgin-English speaking boy named Weng, a native of Macao. I had agreed to pay him well, with the understanding that he was to obey me without reasoning why, never to leave my side, and to go wherever I should tell him to go, without questioning motives. So Weng and I went on our pirate woman hunt. When we were almost ready to give up the quest we went to the pier, where a ship was waiting, ready to sail for Hong-Kong.

A few minutes before the boat pulled out I recognized a face among the crowd on the pier. It was one of Madame's crusaders.

He recognized me, too, in spite of my beard. The three of us went back to a *fan-tan* house. Weng, not knowing what it was all about, made furious signs to me to stay away from this man; apparently he knew his reputation.

I brought up the subject of Lai Choi San without delay. Where was she? Was she still in the neighbourhood of Macao? Was she anywhere within reach? I wanted to find her, go along with her again, see her, talk to her.

The pirate replied evasively.

Lai Choi San was somewhere on the West River, near Canton. He, Ping Wong Liu, was captain of his own junk now, armoured to be sure, and doing business of his own, mainly " protecting" fishing-junks from the attacks of pirate ships. This actually meant that Ping Wong Liu levied some kind of a tax on a group of junks whose owners felt safer in having him as a friend when meeting his ship on the high seas. Pretty soon he was going to get another ship or two, and then probably move his " protection " westward, to the mouth of the West River, the pirate-infested waters on the South China coast.

And what did he know about Lai Choi San? Oh, the old lady was all right. The business had been brisk.

No, he did not think she had had anything to do with the piracy of the *Delhi Maru*. He was certain of it. Why? Well, they had been " busy " somewhere else, and he, Ping Wong Liu, had seen her fleet in the West

The poop watch

The powder magazine

River delta about the time the piracy had occurred, near the Cone Island.

But he would be willing to take me north, where he was certain that Lai Choi San's ships were. He could not go at once, but if I could wait a day or two he would be glad to see me and my boy on board. I should bring my own "chow," of course, he suggested, and the price I should have to pay would be forty-three dollars a day. The sum he mentioned was exactly the amount I had paid to Madame on my last cruise with her, and he seemed to know all about it. It was an exorbitant price, and I tried to bargain, but without success. So finally I agreed.

Two days later I climbed aboard, despite Weng's protests that we were surely going to be butchered in due course of time. But he was loyal enough to hang on to me, and a good cook he proved to be—the gods be thanked !

This junk was considerably smaller than Madame Lai's flagship, on board which I had had the rare opportunity to travel before. However, she prided herself on carrying nearly as many guns as any of Madame's. This was a newer ship and neater. Her large yellow sails shone with an almost blinding effect, the large iron plates around the gunwales were newly-painted, and the two cannons high up on the poop glistened in the sunshine, while two husky chaps in broad-brimmed hats, armed with rifles and wearing cartridge belts, stood watch near the small third mast at the stern, ready to sound an alarm at the slightest provocation, should another pirate junk or peaceful fishing-boat appear round the boulders of the next island.

Right in the middle of the craft was the powder

magazine. One of the men, an ugly, copper-coloured gentleman, who had seen many battles and whose two front teeth had been left on the deck of an enemy junk, offered to open the hatch and show me the yellowish powder bags, made of grass and neatly piled on the shelves. He also dragged forth an antiquated collection of cannon-balls and shot, supposed to fit the museum pieces on the deck. There was no mistake about it—if any of the larger shots should hit the hull of a junk, *that* junk would be due at Davy Jones's locker immediately.

*   *   *   *   *

We sailed out of Macao harbour and headed for Bias Bay. The morning passed uneventfully. I lay upon the deck at my ease, stretched out in the shadow of a sail, my head pillowed upon my camera case. Shortly after noon we entered enemy waters and I got up, but still nothing happened. We might have been sailing on some lake in the Garden of Eden, so far as any appearance of danger was concerned.

An island loomed up to starboard, and the look-out in the bows took soundings with a long bamboo pole. Soon the island appeared very clearly, and the junk steered directly towards it. The crew made ready to let the medieval stone anchor go, but before they dropped it overboard we were all thrown off our feet by a terrific jolt. I thought the masts would crash down and the whole ship break up.

We had grounded high and securely on one of those treacherous sand-banks which sometimes form over-night on the lee side of the islands in the river deltas. The confusion finally ended, and we soon discovered that only high water or a change in the currents could make the sand-bar release its grip on our ship. So the men lighted joss-sticks to their deities and burned fire-crackers to scare the devils in the sea. What a noise it was !

The men got the dinghy ready, and half the crew and my boy got into the boat. I took my camera and went ashore with the men. It was now late in the afternoon, and it was obvious that we were going to stay here over-night waiting for high tide and favourable currents.

The island was very rocky, with one high hill at its centre. The total area probably did not exceed half a square mile. I decided to scale this hill, ostensibly to look at the beautiful sunset, the surrounding islands, and the adjacent waters, but really to get my bearings and to learn if we were in immediate danger. On the slopes of this hill was a joss-house—a little temple—with an idol and a few sacred vessels in which to burn incense. However idyllic this little temple was, I had to leave it and climb on up the hill. When my boy and I reached the top the sun was just setting.

There below us was our ship. And a short distance seaward two swift-sailing junks were approaching her.

Were they enemies or friends ? We would soon find out. Our ship had lowered her sails, and anyone not in the secret would have been unable to tell that she rested helplessly and immovably on a sand-bank.

Now they had come within shooting distance, but not a shot was fired ; apparently everything was all right, because I did not see the crew ashore make any efforts to rush back to the ship. So they were friends, thank God ! To be sure, two boat-loads of men pulled away from the new-comers, who also lowered their sails. It seemed a miracle that they were not aground too. Just our ship's bad luck.

The crews had joined our men ashore and had started huge bonfires by the time I descended the hill. There were also women ashore, as all junks carry women to cook the men's food ; they sat apart, while the men jabbered away for all their Cantonese tongues could stand.

They talked excitedly, and I imagined that the looks they gave me were not over friendly. But why ?

When I went on board I saw that something unusual was happening. Our captain gesticulated and talked and explained something to two men who were apparently the captains of the other two junks. The women and some of the crew stood by and listened with evident interest ; but as soon as we stepped on deck they all turned towards us, and I had a sickening feeling that I had been the subject of the discussion. The men sneered when they saw us, but I tried not to pay any attention and climbed the poop, where I lay down and told Weng as nonchalantly as I could to find out from the captain what all the row was about.

He soon came back with the bad news. It seemed that the other sea-faring gentlemen were some sort of partners of our captain, and that they had accused him of trying to kidnap me, which our captain flatly denied, of course. He referred the matter to me, but the other two slant-eyed rovers only sneered. They demanded that I should move over to their ship. This, of course, I refused to do. Weng explained that the partners had suspected our captain of doing some private kidnapping business without letting them in on it.

Whether or not Ping Wong Liu, the captain, was wrongly accused, the situation was not pleasant ; after all, to be kept a prisoner for ransom was not at all in my

Our junk aground on a sand-bank

The captions conferring over their " chow "

A typical pirate type

programme. Nor was it authorized by the editors of the publications for which I write.

But it transpired soon that they did not wish to hold me for ransom, but only to be sure that their partner did not double-cross them.

We all had our " chow " together, the Chinese captains, Weng and I. It looked as though we were all very friendly again. The incident seemed to be settled. The peace of the night came with the twinkling stars, and soon the splashing of the waves against the hull and an occasional loud snore were the only sounds to break the stillness.

But the incident was not closed.

The tide lifted our junk from the sand-bar, and I was certain that we were going to proceed. Weng had gone forward. One of the other captains had come over at an unearthly hour and had had a long talk with the master of our ship. He came to me and Weng translated.

" Master, he say we go top-side."

" Top-side ? " I did not understand.

" Go ashore. I donno why go shore."

" Go shore, stay joss - house — bye - bye he come back — fetch Lai Choi San ——— " (Or words to that effect.)

I did not like this at all. We would be put ashore and kept prisoners in the temple until he went all round the South China Coast to find my Lady Piratess. No, I did not like it at all.

Still, there was not very much we could say for ourselves, although I raved a good deal in my very best pidgin-English, in which I was not any too well versed. But the men meant business, and in a few minutes

I

Weng and I and five other men were rowed away in the dinghy and our procession led straight up to the temple.

Half-way up the path to the hill I turned round. The man immediately behind me grunted and gave me an unfriendly push. I had caught a glimpse of two junks steering off shore. One had bright yellow sails. It was our junk! I had never seen any of my men before. They did not belong to our crew.

There was the temple.

Weng and I were pushed in.

*   *   *   *   *

They changed guards once a day.

On the third day our food supply gave out. Weng argued for permission to go on board the remaining junk to get food, but the guards only shouted at him. But they had not taken any of my belongings nor asked me for money or valuables. They asked for cigarettes, but as I was a non-smoker I could only show them that I did not own any to give them. Maybe they did not believe me. Their treatment grew harsher every hour—a bad sign, I concluded.

About three o'clock in the afternoon there was a great deal of excitement among our guards. Weng ventured to ask what it was all about. To our surprise they asked us to come out of our prison, and the leader pointed at a large sail, in fact three of them, swooping straight down upon our island. We could see the dinghy pull out from the anchored junk, and three of our guards ran excitedly down to the beach. The remaining two men became highly nervous, babbled all the time in high-pitched falsetto and gesticulated. Half-way to the shore the dinghy swung round and hurried back to the junk. The junk had set her sails and was already swinging out of the bay, when the big new-comer hove to around the farthermost point of the island, but still too far away to use the antiquated cannons which she carried. The junk fled in a panic, leaving the five guards behind. They were panic-stricken by this time too.

For Weng and me this was a critical moment. Five infuriated Chinese pirates armed to the teeth could do anything they wished to us. I motioned to Weng to go back to the temple, which he did in an admirably casual manner. In the meantime the large junk had let go her anchor, and two boat-loads of men pulled out.

Then I bolted for our little sanctuary. There was a heavy hard-wood door which I barely had time to shut, for the guards were right at our heels. Weng grabbed the table which was used as an altar and we barricaded ourselves. The guards shouted and knocked furiously at the door with their rifle butts. I expected them to begin a fusillade at any moment, but nothing happened. The knocking and the shouting stopped too.

However, after a few minutes I heard some shots. They sounded as though they were some distance away. There were some huge rocks a few hundred yards east of our refuge, and it sounded as though the shots came from there.

Finally we decided to open the door. Nobody was in sight, and Weng and I walked out. Very careful we were, lest someone should spot us and take a shot at us. We stood behind a clump of trees gazing at the boulders, where the shooting was still going on, until we were suddenly startled by a loud bang—it was the temple door which someone had slammed.

Then the men from the new junk came forth, one after another. We signalled them to advance as we had no arms, and they came.

Greatly astonished to see that some of them wore Chinese army caps, I asked who they were. Also why they had come.

The leader explained to Weng that they had heard of a white man who was being held for ransom, and that they did not want Ping Wong Liu or anyone else to do that sort of thing. I told Weng to explain that we had not been kept for ransom, but had " booked passage " on the first junk upon the promise of Ping Wong Liu to bring us to the ever-moving abode of Madame Lai Choi San. I was an old friend of hers, I bragged, at the same time praying to my lucky stars that this gang would be friendly to her also.

Eight men now came slowly out of the natural rock fortress where my recent guards had fortified themselves, and the blighter inside the temple was dragged forth. His knees were shaky and his hands could not reach high enough. I photographed the gathering of his captors and himself as they backed him against the wall with his hands up. Then they shot him down, and the captain gave the order to march.

As I plodded down to the beach with my " rescuers " it dawned upon my now rather tired mind that, after all, what had happened to us was only that Weng and I, as commercial commodity—prospective ransom-bringers— had changed hands for the third time, and that this was the end of our chase after Madame.

We went aboard the junk—again one of those gloriously armoured, prehistoric monsters. The captain met us, and he struck me at once as a likeable chap.

Temple Island: taking away the prisoner

The rocks among which my rescuers fought [132

Serious business: the execution of one of the men at the temple

He shook hands cordially and spoke in fairly good English.

"Solly. You fliends of Si Nai Lai?"

Si Nai is the Chinese for Mrs.

"Yes," I confirmed. "Where is she? I want to see her."

"She Canton," he said. "She my cousin. I take you shoreside—you take boat Canton. I give you chit. You see her Canton."

It further transpired that Ping Wong Liu had known all the time that Madame Lai was in the city of Canton and not on the West River, as he had told me. He could have given me this information had he so desired, and I should have taken the first boat for Canton, which is only ninety odd miles north of Macao. When his "partners" heard that I was on Ping's junk they were sure that this gentleman had tried to double-cross them in some way, as he had not mentioned anything about me to them, and they thought that he intended keeping what ransom money he could get out of me for himself. Which was probably all wrong. When Lai Choi San's relative, or cousin as he styled himself, heard about this through the underground channels of their remarkably efficient intelligence system, he had decided to get into the game himself, he admitted. Hearing, however, that I was probably the same man who had sailed earlier in the summer with this Queen of Pirates, he changed his mind and helped me out of a rather unpleasant situation. For which I was truly grateful.

They took me to the nearest point on Lappa Island, and after a few hours' walk I was back in Macao, where a couple of days later my new acquaintance looked me up at my lodgings and handed me a chit to his piratical relation in Canton, the Lady Piratess, Lai Choi San.

*　　*　　*　　*　　*

The Riviera Hotel is a modern establishment, and a surprisingly well-managed one for a one-horse town such as Macao. As a matter of fact, it isn't logical to call Macao a one-horse town, because there is not a horse in the city.   Transportation is either by rickshaws or automobiles, and men are the beasts of burden.   It is only during the racing season that a few ponies are brought over from Hong-Kong or from Shanghai and kept within the racecourse.   What really would happen to a horse if one should stray on to the streets of Macao it is impossible to say.   More than likely it would be mobbed by curious throngs of Chinese.

However, the Riviera Hotel has a very good bar, where the officialdom and the young Chinese gallants of Macao congregate every evening as a matter of course, either to play billiards or to imbibe their whisky and sodas.   It is a favourite meeting-place of the European sailors, sea-captains, and sometimes of a few officers in the Chinese Customs.

These Customs officials have an ungrateful task to perform—that of guard duty along the coast of China Proper.   Many true adventure stories could be written of their experiences.   Many of them are so strange and fantastic that if they were published they would be disbelieved and scouted as pure fiction.

They are a strange bunch of men, most of them thirty to fifty years of age—well-built, strong, solid fellows who do not brag about their adventurous exploits. It is difficult to get them to talk.

These men are situated in what is probably the most

dangerous part of the whole China coast, a section that is infested with professional smugglers, pirates, and other bandits who would welcome any opportunity to cut the throats of the Customs men and sink their craft. They have engaged in scores of battles about which the world has never heard, and some of these chaps would be covered with wound-stripes had such decorations been given for injuries received in the performance of their "peace-time" duties.

But sometimes in the evenings, when a group of them are sitting round a table, hot rum, sugar and lemon will loosen their tongues ; and when one starts to tell his experiences the next man will join in, and a third will probably find that his experiences have been even stranger. Thus their stories gradually come out.

It was in this way that I first learned of one of the most unusual characters that I was to meet among the pirates. I had joined a party in the second round of rum, and at the fifth I heard the strange story of Ko Leong Tai, the dog-man.

*   *   *   *   *

In the village of Chung King, far up the Yangtze River, lived a very rich merchant named Ko Leong Tai. Since it is in the programme of every wealthy Chinese to be kidnapped sooner or later, there is always a certain sum of money laid aside to be used for ransom. This fact the pirates know well. So it happened that Ko Leong Tai fell into the hands of pirates. The merchant did not worry over much, but promptly sent one of the bandits to his brother with a letter asking that the requested sum be paid. He was certain that the matter would be attended to without delay.

But it was not. The brother decided that it would
be to his interests to see to it that Ko Leong Tai remained
a captive. So he appropriated all the unfortunate
man's property and wrote a letter to the bandits
requesting them to keep his brother a prisoner, and
promising to pay a certain monthly sum for his upkeep.
Ko Leong Tai was then put into a bamboo cage just large
enough for him to squat within. The top of the cage
was set upon greased upright columns, so that its entire
weight rested upon poor Ko Leong Tai's shoulders. Any
attempt upon his part to shift his position only resulted
in bringing the pressure down upon some other part of
his body.

For fourteen years this unfortunate merchant sat in
his cage. In the meantime his body grew deformed and
hideous, and when he was released during the revolution
which overthrew the power of the Mandarins he could not
stand upright, but walked along on all fours like a dog.

He is still alive to-day, and he still walks on all fours
—this dog-man.

But during those fourteen years he had time enough
to plot revenge on his greedy brother, who in the meantime had moved over to Macao. There he had become
interested in a syndicate which had been granted the
gambling monopoly of this Portuguese colony. He is
said to-day to be a very wealthy man indeed. But it is
rumoured that he never dares to leave his house without
being surrounded by a bodyguard, because of his fear of
the avenging arm of the ill-treated brother.

The dog-man was said to have joined a gang of pirates
somewhere around Canton. It had taken him years to
move from his old haunts near Chung King, on the
Yangtze, down to South China, but he had done it.

The man who told me the tale little realized that a few weeks later I would meet the very same dog-man under circumstances almost as strange as those he had related.

*   *   *   *   *

Weng came in one day highly excited.   He said that he had met somebody who knew that I wished to get hold of Lai Choi San, and that this informant had brought news that she was in Canton.   So Weng and I combed all the twelve *fan-tan* dens of Macao, searching for this man.   We did not find him.

At two o'clock in the morning I returned to the hotel, and I found that a friend, a constable of the Macao Police Force, No. 222, was sitting there asleep in a chair. Siwa, the policeman, and I had struck up a friendship, and he brought me much information which I probably never could have obtained without his help.   I shook him by the shoulder, and he woke up.

" What's up, Siwa ? "

He aroused himself quickly and babbled incoherently about meeting a Chinese who had told him about some other Chinese who wanted to get hold of me.   He was certain that the man was a pirate.   Now Siwa did not know of my former relations with the pirates, and the word sounded like blood and murder in his ears.   The good soul wanted to warn me, and he had gathered a lot of details which later turned out to be invaluable.

A Chinese detective had overheard in a den two opium-smokers discussing a foreigner who had been in " partnership " with the unconquerable Lai Choi San, and they had plotted to get hold of me in one way or another.   Whether it was to make away with me or to offer me a chance to join them he could not say, but he suggested that I should be very careful. Meantime he promised to try to get more data. He went away satisfied that he had saved my life for the time being.

The following night I took Weng along, and we boarded a steamer for Canton. It was the usual kind of river boat, protected by grilles with armed guards posted on all the decks, and the third class passengers locked below deck behind bars. I had decided that if I could not join Lai Choi San in Canton I would try to get hold of other gangs, and to that end my rugged appearance probably would be helpful.

It was a beautiful moonlight night, and I sat on deck watching the golden path on the water. Occasionally a dark shadow of a junk passed by, and the contours of the hills stood out black against the dark green night-sky.

A huge guard strolled up and down the deck. At last he stopped beside me. After a time he took out a package of cigarettes, offered me one, and lighted one for himself. In the match's flare I recognized him.

" I beg your pardon," I said, " are you Captain M—— ? "

He wheeled around.

" Yes, I am. How do you know ? "

I told him that we had met before. It was in the autumn of 1927. He had served with the White Russian forces in the Northern Chinese army with the troops of Marshal Sun Ch'uan Fang as a captain on board an armoured train. He remembered me at once. He forgot about his guard duty, put away his rifle, and sat in the rattan chair nearby. We talked for a long time about our experiences.

After the defeat of the Northern forces he had fled with the rest of the Russians to Mukden, and from there

to Harbin. In Harbin he had narrowly escaped falling
into the hands of the Bolsheviks, and had fled to Dairen.
From there he had taken a berth on an Italian steamer
bound for Australia, but had jumped ship in Hong-Kong ;
then, rather than go hungry or beg, he and a few
comrades whom he had met in Hong-Kong had decided
to accept the meagre pay of anti-pirate guards on board
this river boat. Now he was receiving thirty-six Chinese
dollars a month.

" What are your duties on board ? "

He smiled.

" We are supposed to fight the pirates should any
attack be made on the ship."

" What are the chances of an attack ? "

"Not very great," he confided, "because the company
pays tribute to the pirates."

" What do you mean ? Do the pirates actually
receive regular sums in return for keeping their hands
off this ship ? "

" You don't seem to believe me, but I'll tell you what
happened only two weeks ago. The owners of this ship—
they are Chinese—received a letter from a well-known
pirate chief about two months ago requesting that a con-
signment of opium should be brought to a certain point
and thrown into a *sampan* which would be lying nearby.

" This was done.

" A few days later the company again received a
letter requesting that $5,000 in silver coin should be
paid in the same manner ; that is, the money should be
thrown overboard into a waiting *sampan*.

" When it came to cash payment the owners refused
to comply. Everything went well for about a couple of
weeks, when we noticed that the same passengers always

travelled back and forth aboard us between Macao and Canton. It was a bad sign. That meant that more than likely these passengers were pirates, whose business it was to study the ship and the habits of her officers—the usual method. So the captain reported the matter without delay, mentioning also that on each trip we had seen a waiting *sampan* situated at the point where the money was expected to be handed over.

" We are three Russians on this ship, and we were all for fighting it out with the pirates. We begged the captain not to pay any money to the bandits. Meantime we were having our own rehearsals. We Russians are supposed to be Corporals of the Guard ; the rest of the guard are Indians. For the benefit of these travelling Chinese we got hold of a machine-gun and did a lot of shooting and manœuvring, hoping that all this would be reported to the bandit chief. In other words, we hoped that he would get cold feet.

" One afternoon, when we were ready to leave Macao, we noticed an unusually large number of third class passengers—husky and vicious-looking Chinese. Three of them were actually caught with arms concealed under their clothes while boarding the ship. There is a heavy penalty for Chinese found carrying arms or smuggling them on board a ship, so these men were turned over to the police. But something was about to happen, of that we were sure.

" The ship's compradore was frightened out of his wits, and the crew went up to the first mate with the news that there would sure to be an attack by the pirates unless something was done to prevent it.

" Well, something was done about it. A heavy bag was brought to the captain when we arrived within sight

The author after his imprisonment on Temple Island

The men who rescued me from Temple Island
(Note the deserters' military caps)

of the *sampan*. The ship slowed down, the *sampan* approached, and the bag was thrown over into the boat. It was heavy enough to knock the man who caught it off his feet. Frankly, I hoped that the bag would go through the bottom of the tiny craft.

"And thus the tribute was paid. We have had peaceful sailings since. Occasionally we bring some opium to mysterious messengers visiting aboard us in Macao, or some of the crew throw packages overboard to be picked up by *sampans* or junks.

"We are at peace with the bandits, but there is one thing that I don't understand. Why do the Chinese owners insist upon keeping us on board as pirate guards and pay us salaries for it?

"By the way, if you are not too sleepy I would like you to meet my friends, the other Russians. Come to our cabin after midnight."

I accepted the invitation. Down in the cabin of the Russians was a merry vodka bottle standing in the middle of the table, and I was hailed with a loud Russian cheer.

It happens that I speak Russian as well as a native, having spent part of my early childhood in Southern Russia, and it never occurred to them that I was other than a Russian.

We drank tea, we drank vodka, we mixed lemon and jam with our tea, and we sang songs of the Volga and Dnieper. They told me many weird tales, but there was one thing especially that made me prick up my ears— the story of a Chinaman, apparently a pirate or bandit, who had served in the Russian Army during the Russo-Japanese War, probably as a servant to an officer. He spoke understandable Russian and had been in Canton not long before.

There and then I concocted a plan.

I told them exactly what I wanted to do. They were all three enthusiastic to join me in one capacity or another, and go along on my search for pirates. They were all for jumping ship immediately in Canton, and if necessary starting their own pirate gang—why not? But it was the vodka that made them so enthusiastic. They had jobs to take care of. It took a couple of glasses of vodka to convince them of the foolishness of such a scheme, but they agreed to help me carry out my plan.

I was to disguise myself as a down-and-out Russian refugee, put on my worst clothes, and go begging a job among the Chinese junks if necessary. Meantime my new friends would try to hunt up this Russian-speaking Chinese and steer me into his path. There seemed to be possibilities in the plan.

Should I pose as a White or a Red refugee? It would be dangerous to pose as Red, they said, because Reds were hunted mercilessly by the present Chinese Government, and if caught their heads were chopped off without trial or inquiry. Neither did they like the idea of my posing as a White Russian who was down and out. There was a certain pride in those boys, and I admired them for it. We agreed to let circumstances decide the question.

I left them early in the morning and awakened Weng. I found him asleep in one of the lifeboats. The loyal soul had no idea what I was up to, but nevertheless he had hung on to me doggedly. I believe that he liked me, but I could never reconcile him to my camera. He had consistently refused to have his picture taken. In fact, I finally promised never to take his picture. He was in deadly fear of losing his soul.   Once he caught me trying to steal a snapshot of him, and his look of thorough disgust told me exactly what he thought of me.   I never ventured to do it again.   I did not want to break his faith in me.

I broke the news to him that he was going to be a down-and-outer for the next two months.

"Maskee.   Never mind," was all that he said.

I borrowed an empty potato bag and put my supply of film, a pair of shoes, and my camera in it.   The rest of my baggage I left on board the ship with those three good Russians.   As I did not dare to walk off the boat in broad daylight, I stayed in my friends' cabin.   The ship was not to sail before the next morning.

Meantime the man who knew the Russian-speaking Chinese went out to hunt for him, taking Weng with him. At eight o'clock I slipped ashore and found Weng patiently squatting on a bale of merchandise.

"Where is Russian master?" I asked.

"No savee," he said.   "Russian master got drunk speaking top-side Russian-Chinese."

"What do you mean, 'speaking top-side Russian-Chinese'?"

"Chinaman's house top-side."

"You know the way?"

"Yes, master."

"Look here, Weng, quit calling me 'master' for a couple of weeks.   Call me Li."

"Yes, master."   And then he caught himself and said, "Master Li."

Weng had transformed into an ordinary coolie.   He was barefooted, and he wore a sort of knee-breeches, or perhaps he had only rolled up his trousers.   Where he had got hold of the dirty blouse he wore I don't know. Perhaps some of the crew had obliged him. He also wore a straw hat of the Chinese junk-man's 1929 mode, which is the same as that of 1632 or any other year.

I had a torn blouse of indefinite colour, a dirty pair of trousers held up with a piece of string.

" Say, Weng, do you think I am crazy ? "

" Yes, master." And again caught himself. " Master Li."

" Well, go on thinking that I am crazy, and tell everybody about it."

" All lightee, Li." And here we finally became Weng and Li.

*   *   *   *   *

There are few cities like Canton in China. It is a well-built city as Chinese cities go, but many of the streets are so narrow that if one walked with outstretched hands one could touch the houses on both sides. Two rickshaws have a difficult time in passing each other, and a dog fight is enough to stop the traffic. There are hundreds of such streets ; yet the traffic is regulated with a precision that would make a traffic cop on New York's Forty-Second Street and Fifth Avenue feel dizzy. People never collide, and if two rickshaws run into each other, then the pullers curse each other, smile and continue on their ways.

Here are the Canton shawl shops, the jade and ivory shops, and next to them the fan-maker's. Nearby is the kingfisher feather jeweller. The streets and the houses are filled with seething humanity, and the air is saturated with the peculiar, indescribable odour of old Cathay.

We must have walked for miles. My feet hurt. I was not used to walking barefooted, but Weng led the way. He said he knew where he was going, and somehow I had become accustomed to trusting that boy. We turned to the right and passed a fruit stand. Weng said a few words to the shopkeeper, and we entered an open yard which was terribly dirty and muddy because of the rain that had fallen earlier in the day. We crossed the yard and trampled on a squealing pig. Weng opened a narrow door. A sooty lamp burned inside, and I could distinguish a steep and narrow staircase. Weng climbed up and I followed.

It was not without an uncanny feeling behind the shoulder blades such as one experiences as a child when afraid of the dark.

I could not help whispering to Weng: "Are you sure, Weng, that this is all right."

"It is all lightee, ma—Li."

I followed him cautiously. He opened a door. In the dim light of a lantern I saw two men reclining on a couch. The one must have been the Russian-speaking Chinese.

The other was—Chang Liu!

*   *   *   *   *

My heart went cold within me.

Chang Liu did not show any signs of recognition, and neither did I, but I knew instantly that he had recognized me. For some reason of his own he did not want to show that he knew me.

"Who are you?" Chang Liu asked me.

"Litoff, Alexander Litoff at your service, sir."

"You Russian?" interrupted the other.

K

"Yes, I am Russian," I replied.

"*Govorite, po russki ?*"   ("Do you speak Russian ?")
he asked.

"*Konetchno*" ("Certainly"), I answered promptly.

So this was the Russian-speaking Chinese.

"Do you know Georgij, the guard?" the Chinese
asked me in Russian.

"Yes, I know him," I answered. "He told me that
you wanted a bodyguard."

"How much do you want?"

"Food, clothes, and vodka money, and a job for Weng,
my friend here."

"Where do you stay?"   Chang Liu asked in his
perfect English, speaking through the interpreter, and
pretending not to be aware of my knowledge of English.

"Nowhere at present. I just came from Macao."

Chang Liu gave me a queer look and nodded his
head.

Then the two Chinese talked things over for a few
moments. Weng squatted near the door, and anxiously
listened to the conversation. Occasionally they asked
him a few questions. I understood the trend of their
questions, and I also could grasp that Chang Liu
was helping me along.   Then he turned to me and
said: "I want you to come with me. You will get
a job."

And then we three, Chang, Weng and I, walked out,
leaving the Russian-speaking one alone.

When well outside he said a few words to Weng,
who instantly disappeared.

*   *   *   *   *

For a long time we walked without saying a word,

and then Chang Liu turned to me and in a few words said that I was the most persistent fool he had ever met, and as such deserved to succeed.

"Chang Liu," I asked, " did you send me that message in the prison ? "

He did not answer directly, but gave me another queer look, and said: " Well, I hope you had some use for it."

Then I laughed, and told him in as few words as I could how I had spent three months in jail following his advice to try to get hold of the prisoners whose numbers he had given me in such a discreet way.

He roared with laughter.

"I thought it was a good joke. You are the grandest idiot I have ever met. If only you could see yourself in the mirror right now. Still, I won't give you away. As a matter of fact I need your help. I shall take you to my home, and will arrange for you to go with the man you just met, the Russian-speaking fellow, to the West River."

I almost fell on his neck. Such a promise coming from Chang Liu I felt was an assurance of success, but I racked my brain to figure out what it was that Chang wanted to find out about the West River pirates.

And then Weng appeared with my clothes, which he had brought from the steamer at Chang Liu's order.

"You are to stay with me for two days at least," Chang Liu stated. "While you are here you don't need to wear this costume, but I would suggest that you should not leave this house."

And so Weng and I were virtually prisoners for a

couple of days, during which time we enjoyed Chang Liu's hospitality.

His home was rather elaborate. On the ground floor were some offices, where two clerks sat from morning to night with their noses over account books, writing down endless strings of sprightly dancing Chinese characters. I asked Chang Liu what these two men were doing, but he answered casually: " Oh, they are handling my business."

As he did not appear to want to go into details, I did not press him for further information.

Chang Liu was married, and this was his home ; rather, it was the house where his family usually stayed. I understood that he owned many houses in different parts of China, and I should not have been greatly surprised to learn that he had a wife staying in each of them. Once I ventured to ask how many wives he had. He replied : " I think there are four."

" How many children have you ? "

" O—o—oh, many."

" You must be a rich man, Chang Liu. Why don't you retire and go to Europe ? "

A strange, distant look came into his eyes. For a while he did not answer, then he turned away and said casually : " I can't, but I wish I could."

" Several years ago," he continued, " I was ' blackmailed ' into financing a certain undertaking. I was asked to lend some money to a group of people and was promised a good return. I did not know at that time what they wanted the money for. It was paid back to me, and the return was very good indeed ; but the group who had borrowed the money informed me of all the details of their business, and they also said that I was now one of them, and that if I withdrew my financial support they would do away with my eldest son and my wife, and thereafter stamp the whole family off the face of the earth."

" And so you continued the game on the wrong side ? " I asked. He shrugged his shoulders and busied himself mixing ink in a bowl in front of him.

I was shown a room, and Weng was instructed to keep a watch so that nobody should enter it unless in Chang Liu's company.

It was a large room with rather bare walls and low Chinese furniture. The couch upon which I was to sleep was without a mattress, and for a pillow I was offered the usual Chinese head-rest of porcelain. As the nights were rather cold, two heavy silk coverlets were brought in. If I wanted anything to eat or to drink when Chang Liu was not present I had only to clap my hands and convey my wishes to Weng, who would translate them to one of the many servants in the house.

* * * * *

On the second day things began to happen. The Russian-speaking One appeared, and he seemed somewhat surprised at my transformation. Chang Liu explained that he had supplied my clothes, and that seemed to satisfy the other's suspicions.

We drank bitter green tea, and Chang Liu advised me that after sunset he would take me up the river to see a Number One man whom he expected to find on a " flower boat." This man would decide whether or not I was to get the job as bodyguard.

" Whose body am I to guard ? " I inquired.

" You will find out about it later. It is no use to tell

you before you know whether you are going to get the job or not."

I nodded assent, and the matter was dropped.

But I was far from satisfied. I felt very uneasy. I did not like the idea of being dragged aboard a " flower boat," one of the many floating brothels anchored along the Canton River and patronized by the shifting population of junkmen, *sampan* hands, pirate chiefs, American and British bluejackets, and occasionally a foolish tourist who finds his way to them in his search for excitement and something " unusual." Almost anything may happen and frequently does happen aboard these craft. I did not like the prospect. That night Chang Liu, the Russian-speaking One, Weng and I walked over the little bridge spanning a canal which separates Shameen from Canton.

What a difference between these two cities ! Canton is busy, humming with the doings of labourers and all the million different noises of its Chinese population, while Shameen is a dignified, well - built and rather modern city, with broad, tree-covered boulevards, banks, numberless consulates, and a good hotel. Snappy, uniformed Frenchmen and Englishmen and occasionally a few Japanese sailors are to be seen strolling along the boulevards, while American sailors hang about the few bars and restaurants.

We walked through Shameen, and on the water-front hailed a wiggling *sampan*. We jumped in and the oarsman shoved off. The tide was strong, and we sped past hundreds of anchored junks and barges until finally the " flower boats " loomed in front of us. In a few minutes we were aboard one of them and being greeted by a grinning old woman. Like all of the other craft of

*The native quarters and Shameen (the foreign settlement)
in Canton are separated by a canal*

Among the junks of Canton

The "flower boats" of Canton

its kind, it was a gaily-decorated barge comprising a restaurant and the quarters of the attending "ladies."

Chang Liu asked after the Number One man whom we were going to meet, and the woman nodded and replied that he was waiting.

Two girls, hardly more than children, appeared and squatted on the floor. Soon another girl brought musical instruments, and they began to sing a monotonous melody. I thought the performance was atrocious, but Chang Liu and the Russian-speaking One and Weng, who had learned to act as one of us rather than as a servant, seemed to enjoy it immensely.

The Russian-speaking One turned to me and said : "*Ochen horosho*" ("Very good").

"*Dlja menja, kak jevr opeitzu, trudno ponjat kitaishuyu musiku*" ("For me, as a European, it is rather difficult to understand Chinese music").

The remark passed over the head of the Chinese, who probably accepted my words as a general criticism, meaning that I did not care for the performance of the girls.

Then the Number One man appeared. In stature he was somewhat smaller than the Russian-speaking One, who really was a giant among the diminutive Chinese. He was an elderly man, perhaps fifty. He smiled at me in a friendly manner, and then we sat down to eat.

The Russian-speaking One addressed me in Russian, Chang Liu spoke to me in English, and Weng used his delightful pidgin-English ; then we all spoke together. It seemed that the conversation was not going to end successfully for me, because the man shook his head emphatically when Chang Liu pointed at me and asked a question. I knew that I had been rejected as a bodyguard. Then Chang Liu ordered rice wine, and we drank.

The Chinese became gay after one cup, while I had three cups and felt anything but gay. The Chinese wiped perspiration off their foreheads and grew pink and scarlet, but to me the wine seemed very mild. Chinese cannot stand much alcohol. When they had drunk three glasses, and I seven or eight, we became quite merry. Then Chang Liu began to plead earnestly in my behalf again.

But I had been mistaken about that wine ; it was very treacherous. The room grew dim, and then the smiling faces of the Chinese began alternately to grow large and then very small. Sometimes they would disappear altogether. But I remember distinctly the Number One man smiling at me, and the Russian-speaking One telling me that matters had been arranged by the influential Chang Liu, that they did not want to see a friend of theirs starve or go begging, and that since their friend the chief of the West River pirates had needed a bodyguard for some time, the Number One man would take me along. I would get rice and occasionally a few dollars—and clothes if anything large enough for me could be found—but he made it clear that they had no use for Weng, my Chinese friend. We were going to sail the next day at sunset.

Weng was worried. He wanted to go too, and finally he asked my permission to sneak on board. I told him that he not only had my permission but also my orders to do so. That seemed to please him highly.

*   *   *   *   *

Next day I put on my " working outfit " and told

Weng to get into his. Then Chang Liu walked with us to the den of the Russian-speaking One. He looked displeased at the sight of Weng, and they talked excitedly for several minutes. I told Weng to offer himself as a servant in exchange for food. I told him to explain that our friendship was so great that, rather than be separated, he would die. Even pirates can be sentimental, and there was a soft look in the Russian-speaking One's eyes when he had heard the beautiful speech of the faithful Weng. So it was decided that Weng should go along. This was a much better solution than I had expected. To sneak aboard a pirate junk is not good form. Serious complications can result afterwards for the delinquents.

I had imagined that we were going to board a junk similar to Lai Choi San's ship, but instead we rode in a *sampan* for about half a mile up the Canton River and there boarded a sort of house-boat filled with Chinese. We waited for two hours for a tug-boat, and then we were off. Chang Liu left us as soon as we had got aboard the boat, and the Russian-speaking One, the Number One man, Weng and I were assigned a small cabin together. An attendant came in at once and asked if we wanted to smoke opium. Weng and I refused, but the two others ordered their pipes and the lamp.

We were on our way.

PART SIX

WE proceeded slowly. The tug-boat was an old-fashioned affair with an engine which puffed and whistled at each turn of the propeller. The tide was against us.

There was a large room in the middle of the boat, and on top of it the passengers, consisting of Chinese men, women and children, made themselves at home. In the stern was the kitchen, but what dirt, grease and filth! The rice was cooked in a black iron pot, and I shuddered at the thought of eating such food. It was a long trip to Chang-Men, our destination, and if I did not take any food, I would be very hungry before we got there.

It is such a craft as this that the West River pirates love to hold up. At places where the river is narrow the pirates post themselves and subject the house-boats to fusillades. Sometimes the boats pass with the passengers unharmed, but very often the bandits succeed in stopping the barge and boarding it. The programme is the old one : the passengers who resist are killed and the prosperous-looking ones are held for ransom.

The Chinese travellers know very well that they take those risks, and they dress accordingly. At first glance it seemed a scurvy-looking group of voyagers who had boarded this ship, but judging from their manners many of them were wealthy and probably well educated, some of the younger women especially. Their hair was exquisitely dressed, and they could not resist the temptation to wear beautiful jade rings in their ears. Still, they wore the common black dresses of working-women, but their rough sandals did not at all suit their dainty, carefully-pedicured feet.

At three o'clock in the morning we were going to pass one of the narrow straits where an attack was likely to be made, and the coxswain and one of the attendants suggested that we should lie on the deck, because if the pirates should begin shooting at the boat the deck would be the safest place. We thanked him profusely, but when the time came for us to go to bed the Number One man and the Russian-speaking One lay down on the couch.

" Aren't you going to lie down on the floor ? " I asked.

The Russian-speaking One favoured me with a sarcastic smile, and translated the question to the Number One man. He grinned.

" Aren't you afraid that pirates are going to shoot at this boat to-night ? " I continued.

" No pirates will shoot at this boat to-night," he said.

And so I slept on my bunk, and woke up early next morning at dawn.

In a few hours we would be in Chang-Men.

*   *   *   *   *

Some of the passengers began to stir. The young women made themselves up, the mothers washed the faces of their youngsters, and the old women started the charcoal fire in the stern and boiled their tea. Soon the steaming rice-pots were ready to be passed round. Breakfast resembled a sleight-of-hand performance, and when it was finished the deck was littered with egg-shells.

There was a sharp smell of dried squid, mixed with the fumes of cheap tobacco.

I was now very hungry, but the sight of the dirty rice bowls and the equally dirty rice and the odorous squid took away my appetite. I decided to wait until we landed in Chang-Men before eating.

Weng came up to me. It was the first opportunity I had to talk with him in private.

"Well, Weng," I said, "are you sorry you are going with me?"

He hesitated, then managed a "No-o-o, but I think Macao better. Better chow, better sleep."

"Oh, you are quite right about that. By the way, what have you found out about these two men with us? What do you know about the Russian-speaking One?"

"He no belong pirate yet. He belong Master Chang Liu. He say he know you from Tientsin."

"Good thing you told me that. You send him over to me, and keep the Number One man from interrupting us."

"Yes, Mast—— Li."

*   *   *   *   *

I thought Chang Liu should have told me more about the Russian-speaking One. On the other hand, perhaps he wanted the man himself to tell me his story. I rather think he did not want me to know how deeply he was implicated in this business, if it was his "business."

The Russian-speaking One came over, and we had a long talk.

"Who is the man I am going to serve?" I asked.

"The man I am also going to serve," he replied.

"That isn't an answer. I want to know who is going to be my boss."

"Oh, he is a very strong chief. He has many warriors under his command. . . ."

"Is he an officer, a military leader, a *tuan* ?"

"No, he is not, but he has men of his own."

"Let us be frank about this," I went on impatiently. "Is he a brigand ? Or is he starting a revolution of his own ? Let me know something about him. What is his name ?"

"His name is Wong Kiu."

"Wong Kiu !"

I had heard about this man. He was known to be the most ferocious bandit in the whole West River region. I had learned about him from a Macao missionary who had dared to sail on his mission of Gospel into this bandit's realm, and who for some reason had been spared and had come out alive.

So we were going to the village of Fu San ! What was Chang Liu's idea of sending me there ?" I asked the Russian-speaking One outright. "Does this strong man really need a bodyguard ?"

"Yes, he wants a man he can trust. He needs ten men—not one."

"I should think so with the reputation he has."

"Oh, he is not a bad man," he hastened to explain. "He only robs the rich and gives the money to the poor."

"Of course he robs the rich. Have you ever heard of anyone robbing the poor ? No sense in that, is there ?"

"No," he replied meditatively, "no sense in that. You are right. But few men give their money to the

poor. He pays for many a poor family's upkeep in
Fu San. And they love him like a god."

Come what might, I was on my path to adventure
all right. At least I knew what I could expect. Weng
came carrying our sack with my shoes, the camera, and
the film hidden in the bundle of ragged clothes.

"Are you making yourself ready to step ashore?"
I asked him jokingly.

"Oh no, not yet, Li, but some man try to steal our
bag. A poor man's bag, but Chinese believe something
because you white man."

I said no more. I understood that he wanted to keep
the bag under his eyes, and let him have his way.

Then we came to Chang-Men.

*   *   *   *   *

We spent the night in a dirty hut hidden in a bamboo
grove a few miles outside the town. It was a one-room
bamboo hut, with chickens roosting on the window-
sills. Bats flew in and out, and the mosquitos came in
hordes.

There was not much sleep for me. The men were
snoring, and I was very hungry, having eaten nothing.
I don't think Weng had had anything to eat either.
Nobody had offered us food, and I was too proud to ask
for any. There was some money in my bag, but I did
not want to show it. It would not have been in keeping
with our role of poor hungry beggars.

I got up the next morning with a splitting headache.
I complained to the Russian-speaking One that I was
hungry. Without a word he went out, and returned
ten minutes later with a wonderful steaming bowl of
rice. Dirty or not dirty, I ate it, and so did Weng.

When dawn came I saw that we were not very far from the river, perhaps not over half a mile. A large *sampan*, with two men asleep on board, had been pulled ashore, but they jumped up and got their boat ready as soon as the Number One man, the Russian-speaking One, Weng and I arrived.

A few minutes of heated conversation followed. Apparently two of us were not expected, but nevertheless the Number One man commanded us to help push the boat into the water. We obeyed. Then we climbed aboard. It was a cold morning, and I was half frozen, so I suggested that I should help to push the boat. The boatmen grinned and nodded for me to go ahead. In an hour we were in midstream ; then the tide got hold of us. The light craft almost flew over the surface.

The banks of the river at this point are low and swampy, and from the dense clumps of flags and cat-tails myriads of frightened ducks arose at our approach.

Weng had fallen asleep in a corner of the boat, faithfully keeping his hands upon the treasured bag ; and I had plenty of time to try to figure out a plausible explanation which would account for the fact that I, a hungry Russian officer and refugee, should be carrying a kodak worth at least two hundred Chinese dollars. If that camera were found it would be a perilous situation indeed. Chinese are notably suspicious about such things.

The higher the sun rose the warmer the day, and I soon grew tired of helping the boatmen. I got a splinter under one of my toe-nails which pained me greatly. Finally, I asked one of the boatmen to lend me his knife so that I might extract the splinter.

Noticing that Weng had stirred in his slumber, I

called out to him. He jumped up at once. We climbed up in the bow where nobody could hear us, and while apparently busied with the splinter I said : " When we come to Fu San the first thing you do is to get my camera and film and bury them in some place where we can easily find them again. If the pirates find out that we have a camera with us our heads will be chop-chop."

He understood perfectly.

" All lightee, Ma—— Li," and then I knew that the matter would be attended to perfectly. Weng was a man of few words and marvellous efficiency.

*   *   *   *   *

Sometimes we heard the sound of gongs, interspersed with string music and songs. Occasionally we passed a water buffalo submerged to his nostrils in the muddy water, only raising his head to snort at us as we passed.

The men had now rigged up a sail, and a good stern wind carried us along with double our former speed. Just before noon we crossed over to the east bank and turned into a little creek. We had hardly stepped ashore when we were hailed by a sentinel, who came striding toward us, rifle in hand, with cartridge belts strung around his waist and over his shoulders. He parleyed with my companions for a moment, and then sat down with us, and pointing to me, asked who I was. To this question the Number One man gave some kind of reply which I did not understand. I asked Weng what he had said, but he shook his head and answered: " Solly, Li, he speakee Hakka ; I no speakee Hakka."

Half an hour later another man came up, took over the duties of the sentinel, while the man who had been relieved rose and disappeared slowly down the creek.

I asked the Russian-speaking One how far we had yet to go. He said that the boat trip had ended, and that we now had only a few miles to march before reaching the village of Fu San, where Wong Kiu resided. The sentinel had gone to inform him of our arrival; meantime we were not to move until we received permission to do so. That made me dubious about the Number One man's importance. If he was really a Number One man in Wong Kiu's service, he surely ought to be known by Wong Kiu's men. On the other hand, I did not know the organization. Perhaps this procedure was merely a matter of discipline. The boatmen sat down, made a fire on the sand, and getting out their pots, boiled their rice. The creek water was used both for cooking and drinking. It was reddish-brown, and apparently alive with algæ. I mumbled a silent prayer to whatever typhoid-preventing gods there be, and dug hungrily into the rice with the chopsticks that Weng had provided me with.

*   *   *   *   *

In the afternoon six men came for us. They were neither rude nor polite, but very much interested in my person. Weng was carrying the sack. He sidled up to me and mumbled: "Everything all lightee. Camera and film all buried."

Heavens! I had even forgotten my order!

"Oh! Where did you bury them?"

"Higher up, where high water no reach them."

"Will you be sure to remember the place?"

"Yes, Ma —— Li."

I gave him a look stern enough to make him remember for the rest of the trip to forget his "Ma ——"

L

We entered the village of Fu San.

Apparently we were expected, and a few of the men seemed to recognize the Number One man. They fell in with him, and walking along with us, talked excitedly. They looked me over from head to heel—not in an unfriendly manner, but silently and appraisingly. I was barefoot, and my feet, unaccustomed to long walks over pebbles and rough ground, hurt me.

Wong Kiu's residence was a real *Yamen*, with two small stone dogs guarding the entrance door. There was a screen inside the gate, and the first living thing that met us was a tremendous black pig — the largest pig I have ever seen, I think, and I have seen a lot of them. There were about a dozen smaller pigs running all around her, but most surprising of all was the soundlessness of this *Sus* family. It struck me as something very strange, and I stopped to take a look at those black beasts. Somebody prodded me in the back and urged me to step on. It was the Number One man.

We walked into a yard through a circular gate, and were told by a man, apparently a servant, to squat down and wait. The Chinese sat upon his heels, and so did I, humble job-seeker that I was supposed to be. But I did not squat very long. My legs grew numb, and I had difficulty in getting up. How the Orientals manage to squat for hours at a time I have never been able to understand.

A strong odour of opium reached us, and Weng whispered: "Big boss, he smoke muchee opium, all time smokee opium."

There was a mangy dog strolling across the yard, and it stole up to me. I did not notice it until the cold nose touched my bare feet, and I jumped. The frightened animal gave a yelp and fled howling into the garden, where it hid itself under some shrubbery and continued to howl as though it had been badly hurt. A woman's voice was immediately raised inside the house. Then the woman, apparently the owner of the voice, came out and reprimanded us for having hurt the poor dog. When she had finished her harangue she beckoned us to step inside, so we followed her. The Number One man told us to wait outside while he himself went in.

We waited for another half hour, and then the Number One man appeared and motioned to us to step in.

Before me stood a far from pleasant-looking, badly scarred, and rather ugly Chinaman. He was of medium height, and he had a striking pair of piercing eyes in marked contrast to the usual inscrutable Oriental eyes. This was Wong Kiu himself.

" What do you want ? " he asked quickly as I entered the room. Those four words were the only English I ever heard him use, and I believe that they were all he knew. I thought at the time, however, that he probably spoke English ; so I ventured into a long description of myself, telling him that I was a Russian refugee, that I had been starving in Shanghai, and that I had been told that he needed a personal bodyguard, and that I hoped that he could give me employment. If he needed a bodyguard I was his man. Surely he could see how strong I was, and in the Russian Army I had learned to fight.

Wong Kiu pursed his lips and regarded me for a long time. I had an uncomfortable feeling that he did not believe me at all.

Then he blurted out a stream of Chinese so rapidly

that Weng could only interpret snatches of it. But those bits were enough to make me understand how I stood in Wong Kiu's estimation.

As a matter of fact, he didn't believe me at all. There was something fishy about a refugee who went about accompanied by a servant, and *what about the camera, and the sack and the many small yellow boxes?* I had a sick feeling in the pit of my stomach. Evidently somebody had examined the contents of our " luggage." However, I asked as nonchalantly as possible : " What bag ? What camera ? And what yellow boxes ? " Wong Kiu clapped his hands and a young servant boy came in. He gave an order, and the boy disappeared, to return a moment later with our sack. Wong Kiu ordered Weng to open it. Weng did so, and out came the contents : a pair of shoes, a torn shirt, a pair of Weng's trousers, and three cans of corned beef—that was all. I had half expected that somebody had unearthed our camera and film and put them back in the sack. Thank goodness ! Nobody had been clever enough to do that.

I could not refrain from making a dramatic gesture which, interpreted, meant : " You see, my friend, somebody has been lying to you."

Wong Kiu's hard eyes bored steadily into those of the Number One man. It was perfectly clear who had been talking. After that Wong Kiu thawed a little, but his manner could hardly have been called friendly. Turning to Weng, he said rather curtly that he did not want me for a bodyguard. However, we were free to go back again if we wanted to, or we could stay if we preferred to do that. No harm would come to us as long as our behaviour was above suspicion. If we did anything that he or his followers did not understand, or if we in any way seemed to betray his hospitality—well—we should have to take the consequences.

That ended the interview.

*   *   *   *   *

The Russian-speaking One, who had been turned out of the house as emphatically as we had been, fell in with us, but I was oblivious to his presence. In fact, I had forgotten all about him. The three of us walked along the street without speaking a word. We felt that the sword of Damocles was hanging over our heads.

The first man who spoke was the Russian-speaking One.

"We must find a boat, a *sampan*, or a junk to take us away from here as soon as possible."

"Look here," I said, irritated at him, "what was your idea in bringing us here? I believed that you were somebody of importance, or at least a friend of these people, yet it seems that Chang Liu has wished you on us for some reason or other."

"Not so loud, master."

"So! It is *master* now! Two days ago it was something else again. Have you also fooled Chang Liu into believing that you were somebody or are you a damned spy of his? I wonder if you know anybody at all in Fu San?"

"Not so loud, master, I never got a chance to speak to Wong Kiu."

"Believe me, brother, you never will. The only thing you can do now is to find us some place to stay over - night and then get us out of here as soon as you can."

He went into the first house we came to and talked

volubly with someone, who finally came out and directed us to another house a short distance away. It was some kind of inn, or perhaps it was a private dwelling ; at any rate, we seemed to be the only guests. We had to go through three courtyards before we came to a room. Three straw mats were thrown in after us. These were our beds. We looked them over, and then Weng and I went out for a walk, leaving the mysterious Russian-speaking One to his own resources.

When we walked out into the street we saw two men armed with rifles enter the house by another gate. Apparently they were Wong Kiu's messengers, and while we strolled slowly along the road I noticed another pair of Chinese following us, keeping some distance away— they were our "shadows." That meant that we had to behave and be very careful. We entered a rice shop, bought some rice with some money which Weng "happened to have," and then we turned back toward our quarters.

Fu San is a prototype of any other Chinese village, a labyrinth of dirty streets swarming with the usual chickens, pigs, and children. Half-grown boys were flying kites, and near by somebody was killing a pig ; at least, it sounded as though pigs were being killed.

We were becoming hungry ; so I told Weng to hurry up and boil a can of corned beef from our sack as soon as we reached the inn. When we re-entered the house, the owner came into the room after us. There was a marked change in his behaviour toward us. He bowed and bowed. The explanation was very soon proffered. Wong Kiu had sent two men to tell him to give me the very best, to put me in a separate room, and to provide me with food, for which Wong Kiu was going to pay him. Furthermore, it appeared that failure on this man's part to make adequate provision for my comfort during my stay in his house would cost him his head. This was indeed rather surprising. I tried to figure out what the trap was.

Perhaps it was the food. Were they going to poison us ? Just then Weng came in with the report that he could not find any tins of corned beef ; somebody had lifted them while we were out. By this time I was certain that we were going to be poisoned. And when the food was brought in on a tray for all three of us, I must admit that I did not touch anything until I had seen the other two taste and swallow their food. When nothing happened during the first ten minutes I decided to brave it. That was a most uncomfortable meal.

Later in the evening I took a look round the premises. The house was filled with people—men, women and a few rather good-looking girls. I asked Weng if they were daughters or servants. He smiled and said " No." They were some kind of sing-song girls staying in this house. This was an inn, and anybody who had the price could rent a room.

Some coolies trotted past, each with two heavy oil-cans filled with water swinging from a pole across his shoulders. Inside the house I could hear a girl's sing-song voice accompanied by some kind of stringed instrument. In the open kitchen three cooks were busy boiling rice and frying chicken, and on a wooden board I saw something which looked very much like eels. Weng, who as usual had kept close to me, ventured to explain: " Those are snakes, Li. You likee ? "

If I had not known that they were snakes I should

have thought them rather delicious looking. Eels appeal to me, and I had decided to taste these at the first opportunity.

The kitchen swarmed with flies, and the hands of the cooks were the dirtiest cooks' hands I have ever seen.

Then I walked out through a rose garden. A beautiful garden it was! A strange contrast to the dirt only a few steps away. There was a pond filled with goldfish — large-finned, lightning streaks of fire. Lazy, floating lotus leaves swung slowly around their stems. A tame white heron stood meditatively on one leg and looked at me suspiciously; then he walked leisurely over to the other side of the pond and gulped down a frog.

I heard footsteps behind me, and whirled around. Soft footfalls in a pirate's garden after twilight do not inspire confidence. But I quickly decided that my nerves were too much on edge. There, following the stone rim of the pond, walked a girl. She smiled at me.

It had been a long time since a girl had smiled at me. And she was a beautiful little thing. I stopped and said to her in English:

"Little girl, you are beautiful! You are just another flower among these roses and this pond, away from dirt and the flies. See those stars in the sky? Let them smile at us! We are children who have forgotten what a smile is; you, a sing-song girl among the bandits, and I—well —— "

Of course, she could not understand a word of it, but she smiled and came up to me. She sat down on an artificial rock, and she threw a stone into the black water, and then I threw one. She threw another, and we both laughed. I took her little hand in mine and kissed it. Frightened, she drew it away. Nobody had ever kissed her hand before. Chinese never kiss.

The night was cold; I decided to shut the window. For a second I stood and looked at the stars. There were millions of them. The sky was dark, and somewhere a dog howled in the distance. The coolies had all gone to sleep. A rooster crowed, and another answered him. Again the dog howled; then I heard footsteps in the yard. I recognized the figure. There was a slight tap on my door. I opened it.

Who says that the Chinese never kiss?

*   *   *   *   *

On the second day Wong Kiu came to visit me. He came in person with a bodyguard of twenty men. To be frank, I was somewhat afraid. That guard of twenty looked suspiciously like an execution squad. Wong Kiu was sullen and unfriendly. He came into my room alone, and the squad waited in the yard. Weng sneaked in, and Wong Kiu told him that he wanted to walk around the village with me. He must have seen the hesitating look in my face, because he smiled reassuringly, and remarked that he wanted to show me everything there was to be seen in the village. Afterwards we should go to his house to have " chow." Then, smiling solicitously, he asked, how I had spent the night.

I thanked him for his attention, and replied that I had slept very well indeed, and that I hoped he was feeling well, and that I trusted his illustrious parents and grandparents were in good health. He replied that

his unworthy mother had a belly-ache, and that his father
was resting comfortably on the opium couch.

Then he asked if I were married, and in such a case
if my boys were all right. We exchanged greetings in
this manner for the next five minutes, and all the time
I was racking my brain in an effort to figure out a means
of escaping what would probably be a rather uncomfortable
situation. But when we came out into the yard the squad
had disappeared.

And then I had a suspicion which later proved
correct. While Wong Kiu and I were exchanging
greetings the squad had taken away the Russian-speaking
One. I never saw him again.

*   *   *   *   *

Wong Kiu, Weng and I walked along the muddy
road. The men whom we met shook their own hands in
greeting, and a group of women with children in their
arms stood in the doorways and looked at us as we
passed.

" Only one other foreign man has been in my village,"
Wong Kiu explained. " He is a missionary, who comes
here once in a while to teach us his religion. You
see the building there ? I let him have it when he is
here."

We walked in. It was a peculiar-looking shack. A
distinct smell of opium came through a half-open door.
Two men were lying on the floor smoking their pipes.
That was the strangest Christian temple I have ever
seen. Wong Kiu bellowed like an ox and flew into a
rage. He kicked among the happy sleepers, and he asked
Weng and me to help throw them out. Of course we
obeyed. We could not very well do anything else. A

small group of men and women who had gathered outside witnessed this feat.

I knew that this intermezzo had definitely established my status as Wong Kiu's friend, and that from then on I could walk safely among the villagers. The tale would spread like wild-fire, I was certain. And I was right. It seems strange that Wong Kiu should have done such a thing as lay hands on his own men. Most assuredly he did not do it on account of the desecration of this chapel. Rather, it was because he had given this house to somebody, and he would not tolerate any usurping of privilege granted even to a foreign devil—and a Christian missionary.

We walked all the way round the village. It was a long walk and the mud was slippery, and my feet were bare. I wondered why I had not put on my shoes, for by this time everyone knew that I had a pair in my sack. Perhaps it was just plain foolishness. Or may be bravado. And then I may have wanted to train myself to walk barefoot. I cannot remember.

A narrow path led down a winding creek, and there we heard hammering and human voices. Apparently Wong Kiu had his own reasons for bringing me there. He wanted me to see this place, and later on, when I had gone on my way, to tell everybody about it.

It was a huge boat-building establishment where scores of men were busy constructing additions to Wong Kiu's navy, which consisted, not of junks, but of long, slender war canoes polished incredibly smooth so that they would cut the water almost without resistance. At least a score of these fighting craft were under construction, and he told me that he had many more at different parts of his territory, all of them manned by well-armed fighting men, and occasionally equipped with machine-guns. These canoes could move almost as fast as a sailing junk in an ordinary wind. And a flock of them armed with machine-guns would be bad medicine for almost anything afloat, short of armed ocean liners.

In action each canoe was manned by twenty to thirty paddlers in the bow and stern, while the space amidships was occupied by fighting men.

By now I felt assured that my life was going to be spared. Wong Kiu went into minute details, telling me of the number of men he was going to have ready for the next season, when he expected to add a lot of territory to his domain. He had a colleague, a neighbour chieftain, farther south ; this man, whose name was Wong To Ping, had a still larger fleet of canoes, and Wong Kiu was doing his best to build a fleet as strong as Wong To Ping's. The old story of the balance of naval power.

*   *   *   *   *

Darkness had fallen when we reached the village. Earlier in the afternoon Wong Kiu had suggested that we were to have dinner at his house. I was not surprised, therefore, to be led across the rice fields where water buffaloes were grazing on the short grass which at this time of the year still clung to the edges of the terraces.

When we finally reached Wong Kiu's house I blessed him for the thought to order water to wash in and hot, perfumed towels for the hands and feet. Then somebody brought slippers for me, and I could think of no more blessings.

He motioned me to follow him, and we again crossed the courtyard and the garden and entered his house. He conversed in a lively fashion with Weng and laughed heartily at some joke. In a little while something occurred, and I made a serious mistake, the consequences of which I felt for a long time afterwards.

Weng and I were ushered into a room and left alone. It was not an elegant room ; on the contrary, it was very simple—almost tawdry. It was probably a kind of servants' ante-chamber. There was a Buddha set away in a corner of the room, with incense burning in a tea-cup full of sand before it. A small ancestral tablet stood near by, and a vase of paper roses, dusty and black, were the only offerings to the departed spirits. A newspaper clipping from a Canton paper and a beer advertisement were pasted on the wall. Two rolls of straw mats lay in the corner. There was no other furniture. The floor was the bare earth.

A man, apparently a servant, came in, took the straw mats and unrolled them in the middle of the floor. They were the kind of mats commonly used for bedding. I told Weng to ask the man what he was doing.

He replied that he was preparing a place for us to eat.

Eat upon those dirty mats ! There must be some mistake. I had been invited by Wong Kiu to partake of his own supper with him. The servant did not know anything about that. At the same moment a girl came in, and brought a bowl of rice and two raw fish, and placed these before us.

This was where I made my mistake. I forgot about my situation. My blood boiled over with indignation. Was this the way to treat a guest ?

I arose and told Weng to follow, and without a word we stalked out of the house. Russian refugee or not, I felt that I was still a white man, and I was not going to be insulted by a Chinaman. I was certain that within a

very short time Wong Kiu would know all about the
indignity we had been submitted to. Surely there must
have been a mistake.

Quite right. Within a few minutes after our return
to the inn a messenger came running. He wanted to
bring us back to Wong Kiu. I refused, and told Weng
to say that unless Wong Kiu came in person and
apologized, he and his band could go to hell. The man
departed with that message.

But Wong Kiu did not apologize; nor did he come
for me.

When I had quieted down I realized that I had made
a mistake which probably would cost me dear.

I had a premonition that Wong Kiu would revenge
himself.

I had slighted him openly, and doubtless the servants
had told all the people in the inn about it. I could hear
them discussing the matter excitedly, and when Weng
came back into the room I told him to keep his eyes
and ears open and report to me anything that happened.
He returned to the room about midnight, and sat down
very quietly, as if he were ready to go to sleep. I
suggested that he share the room with me, and he seemed
glad to do so. I asked him if he had heard anything.
No, he had not. It was as if people had refrained from
discussing this matter of common interest as soon as he
appeared, because they knew that he was implicated.
So Weng and I talked the situation over in whispers;
we knew that Chinese walls have ears even for pidgin-
English.

*   *   *   *   *

There was a quiet rap on the door. I recognized
it. I had entirely forgotten the little girl, who now

walked in. I blew out the lamp and told Weng to stay ; then I asked the girl if she had heard anything about the "scandal."

Oh, yes, she nodded. People were talking about it. Wong Kiu was a terrible person, and she had come to warn us. The best thing was to run away at once. She would be glad to show us the way. In fact, she wanted to go with us. She hated the place, and I had been kind to her. Would I be so good as to take her along with us ?

"Did she know where to find a boat? " I asked. She did not. Then it would be foolish to run away, I counselled, for we would be caught and certainly murdered.

I liked the girl and trusted her. I believed her when she said she was sick of the place and the company. Her miserable life had been forced upon her. She had been sold by her parents for a paltry sum to pay a gambling debt in Macao—not an unusual occurrence— and she wanted very much to see her mother again. She also had a little brother whom she loved dearly, and she was afraid that the older people would maltreat him if she did not return. Wouldn't I please take her along ? I told her, through Weng, that I would take her along when I went. Maybe to-night, maybe to-morrow night, maybe some other night. Meantime she could do some reconnoitring for us. She could go out on the street and see whether or not we were being watched by Wong Kiu's men. She laughed. The whole village was full of Wong Kiu's men, from the innkeeper down to the keeper of the gate. They were all Wong Kiu's men.

The girl came back after a while, whispering to Weng that men were watching the gate. Escape seemed out of the question. I suggested that we should climb to the roof, and try to get out that way, to which Weng remarked, and rightly, that Wong Kiu must certainly have thought of that too. Our only chance was to continue playing the part of the insulted party, come what might.

The girl returned early in the morning, and I instructed Weng as to what I wanted her to do. She should go down to the shore and find out if I could get hold of a *sampan*, and if any junks were expected to enter the little harbour. I whispered to Weng at the same time that he should go with her, if possible, and take a look at our cache. The two departed, leaving me alone.

When I crossed the courtyard people stared at me from every door and window. Nobody smiled at me ; nobody gave me a friendly nod, as they had done on the day before. The atmosphere was strained indeed. It was like waiting for a clock to strike a certain hour, and then—the doom. I certainly felt the seconds tick —and they were slow seconds.

A bowl of rice was brought to me again in the morning, but Weng and the girl had not yet returned. I made signs to the servant who had brought the food, indicating that I wished to wait for Weng, but the man urged me so eagerly that I again became suspicious that the food had been poisoned. Very politely, and with many bows, I suggested that he sit down with me and eat. I expected a refusal, but to my astonishment he accepted the invitation. What a relief ! I filled his bowl with the major portion, and when it had disappeared I then tasted my rice, only to find that I had lost my appetite. Then the servant rushed out for some tea, and I remember that I drank copiously of the brew. One does drink a lot when one is feeling nervous.

Still Wong Kiu did not come to see me. Outside the gate I could see four armed men who never moved from their position. After a time it became unbearable.

Noon came, and Weng and the girl had not returned. What had happened? I decided to take a long chance, boldly cross the courtyard, and walk through the gate.

The four men were there, rifles in their hands and cartridge belts around their waists. As soon as they saw me they got up.

     *   *   *   *   *

What next? I looked at them questioningly, and they returned my stare. They made no attempt to prevent me from passing, so I walked on, expecting every minute to get a bullet in my back. When I was about a hundred yards away I peered cautiously over my shoulder. The four guards seemed not to realize that I had escaped their clutches, for they were slowly loitering along behind me, swinging their guns in a leisurely manner. Apparently they had had orders to guard me, but not to shoot me, nor to harm me in any way.

What a chance to escape! The thought rushed through my brain, but instantly I remembered Weng and the girl. I simply had to walk on. Then to my relief I saw at a distance Weng and the girl. I rushed toward them.

What had happened? What did they know? What had they seen? Was there a chance to escape? When? How soon could we try it? And when was the next junk expected?

The girl was not nervous at all. On the contrary, she laughed at me. The thought of going away probably

M

made her feel happy. She stood in the middle of the open place, and we talked the matter over.

All at once I saw the four guards come into sight. Weng was for running away, but I called him back and said: " If you run away, they will believe that we have guilty consciences ; therefore, stay and let us smile, laugh, and be merry."

Weng told me that he had discovered something which would surely interest me.

What was it ?

He had found a large hut full of prisoners behind bamboo bars. Would I like to see it ?

Prisoners behind bamboo bars ! There was not a single jail in the whole village. They must be captives who were being held for ransom.

I told him to lead me to that house, but to walk slowly, as though we were only loitering aimlessly through these muddy streets. We strolled along, and so did the guards just behind us. We stopped here and there to look at a mud hut, a naked chicken crossing the road, a mah-jongg game going on at a cross-road, a cat washing its face, pigeons circling above us, or at the tall trees shaking their silvery leaves in the breeze. And the guards stopped dutifully each time and looked at those things too, probably noticing them for the first time in their lives.

Weng said : " Two streets more around the corner, and then to the right—that is where the house is."

But we never got there. One of the guards came rushing after us and told us to turn back. We looked astonished, and asked why. He just shook his head, held a rifle in front of us, and told us once more to turn back. And so we turned back !

Now here was something which we were not allowed to see.

A source of considerable income to the pirate clans is kidnapping. They kidnap men, women and children from villages, from raided junks, from the highways along the coast, and from the passenger barges similar to that on which we had arrived in Chang-Men. The price of liberty is entirely dependent upon the presumed riches of the victim. It may be $50; it may be $50,000.

The pirates have "agents" in every town and village of the province, and they supply information regarding the prospective victims, their families — a real and thorough credit information system. And when occasion arises the victim is taken prisoner. I know of cases where even Macanese, that is Chinese living in Macao, have been kidnapped in broad daylight on the main streets of Macao. They have disappeared, only to reappear in a few weeks' time, richer in experience, but with the family exchequer considerably poorer.

I asked Weng if the girl had heard of the ransom prisoners.

She nodded in answer to his question, and stated that she had not only seen them but had actually "entertained" some of them. She remembered one man. He was rather a young chap, a General or something, who had been invited by Wong Kiu to a dinner-party in Shekki. She too had been in Shekki, and she had sung and danced for him. This young warrior had become drunk, doped apparently; at least, he did not wake up until two days later, when he found himself in Wong Kiu's home here in the village. For a considerable time the poor man had been held in a state incapable of knowing whether he was still in Shekki or not. The girl's job had been to keep him entertained whenever he woke up, and, she laughingly admitted, to put him to sleep again.

*   *   *   *   *

We had now reached our inn, and there seemed to be quite a commotion outside. There were more men clustered about, carrying arms, shouting, and gesticulating, and as soon as they saw us approaching they stiffened, calmed down suspiciously, and began to whisper among themselves. The girl was taken aside by one man, probably for questioning.

After a scanty meal I unrolled my straw mat and fell asleep. I did not wake up until late the next morning.

There was no one in the room. A single fly buzzed near the ceiling, occasionally bumping its fat, black body against the panels.

Somebody had opened all the windows, and from the opposite side of the courtyard I could see a group of inquisitive children peeping at me from the wall of the garden.

I missed Weng and wondered absently about him. Usually he was with me, whether I wanted him or not. I went out of the room and asked the first man I saw, in my very best Cantonese where my boy was.

" Peen shue boy ? "

The man shrugged his shoulders and disappeared. Apparently Weng was not in the house at all, and I felt uncomfortable on his behalf. Perhaps he had been taken away for some kind of cross-examination.

So he had.

Wong Kiu had sent a few men for him, and had cross-examined him thoroughly about our " discoveries " of the previous day. Also he had wanted to know about our relationship with the girl. Weng must have been quite frank about the latter question, because Wong Kiu had smiled broadly.

" Well, what did you tell the old robber ? " I asked him.

" I tell him we likee velly much go top-side Macao if we no get job."

Wong Kiu had also tried to discover why I had brought a camera, and what had happened to it. Did I always travel with a camera ? Perhaps I was one of those American reporters about whose escapades Wong Kiu had read in the vernacular papers. Was it true, Wong Kiu had asked, that American writers went to war, flew airplanes, and climbed the highest mountains, and descended to the bottom of the sea just to write about those things ? Apparently Weng did not know, because he had vehemently denied the existence of any such wonderful creatures. At least, he had denied that I was one. Wong Kiu could see for himself that there were no high mountains to climb, no deep seas to descend into, nothing else remarkable about this dirty village. And so far as the camera was concerned, it must have all been a mistake.

Wong Kiu had finally released poor Weng, and here he was—chattering away to me in his pidgin-English, apparently still sound in soul and mind.

*   *   *   *   *

The next morning the girl came in, whispering excitedly that three *sampans* would arrive in the forenoon, and that if we went down to the river we could probably steal a boat and get away. I told Weng and the girl to go ahead to the river, and to play all kinds of foolish pranks to convince onlookers of the harmlessness of their actions. I would appear later. As soon as Weng should get sight of me, he was to hasten to the cache and recover the camera and film.

Weng and the girl went off together about noon. I walked out two hours later. Before leaving I looked into Weng's corner and saw the fateful sack lying on the floor. It would not do to take it along. Still, our only clothes were inside it. I went to the corner, opened the sack, and to my astonishment found another empty sack. Weng had removed the contents, and had left the old sack to allay suspicion. I blessed the boy for his forethought and went out barefooted and whistling, and proceeded in the direction opposite to that which Weng and the girl had taken. A solitary man with a rifle followed me at a distance, but within half an hour I had eluded him. I dodged into an alley and was soon walking westward towards the river. Occasionally I stopped and looked to see if anybody followed me, but as nobody was in sight I continued on my way.

A couple of kilometres or so outside the village I saw Weng signalling to me. As soon as he gained my attention he disappeared shoreward into the brush, from which he emerged a moment later triumphantly dangling my camera-case in his hand, and waving the box containing the film.

There was a *sampan* floating a short distance from the river bank. The girl was sitting in the stern playing with the oar. I ran down the bank, and when I reached the water's edge Weng was aboard. I gave the boat a push, and we floated out to mid-stream.

It looked as though we had escaped.

Men and women wore arms

A pirate fort along the West River

My little friend who escaped with me from Wong Kiu

The river was not very wide here, but one would have had a difficult time swimming across it. The current was swift enough to carry us along at a good rate of speed. I was surprised that nobody shot at us, for we supposed that the theft of the *sampan* would soon be discovered and an alarm spread.

Round the first bend of the river, hidden behind some huge rocks and overhanging vegetation, was a junk just lifting its anchor. Weng suggested that we should steer for it and ask permission to go aboard. I hesitated. There was a row of cannons grinning out through the port-holes like angry watch-dogs, and at the sight of us the crew had stopped their work and begun to look at us with interest. A white man in a *sampan* with a Chinese girl is not often seen in this neighbourhood, and I did not want to attract unnecessary attention. Nobody moved to help us on board, and nobody spoke to us. The silence was almost shrieking. I whispered to Weng to go aboard and speak to the captain. He looked at me hesitatingly, and then gave the crew a " once-over " before he climbed up to the deck.

There were three women on board—all heavily armed. I followed Weng's movements as well as I could from the *sampan*, until I saw him disappear in the cabin below deck. The women came and hung over the rail, gazing stolidly down upon us. I expected Weng to come out at once, but ten minutes passed and he did not appear. I began to feel uneasy. At last a man, carrying a rifle in his hand, climbed out of the cabin and shouted for us to climb up on deck.

I climbed up first, and helped the girl, who was by this time badly frightened. She did not want to follow.

And I didn't blame her. If she had not been in the *sampan*, or if Weng had not been alone in the cabin, I probably would have jumped overboard and swam ashore myself. But now there was nothing to do but obey. Somehow I had a feeling that I was having my last sight of daylight. The pirate in the cabin doorway ordered me to hurry up, and pushed me ahead of him. The treatment was almost as rude as that of a certain warder in Victoria Jail.

The cabin was dark. At first I could not see anyone, but in a few seconds my eyes became accustomed to the poor light, and I saw Weng squatting on the floor. Before him a man crouched on a low chair, knees bent up under his chin, and long monkey-like arms clasping his legs.

I smiled a greeting. It was hard to smile, for I saw the man looking at me appraisingly. His face was not hard ; the eyes were rather sad. His body was terribly thin. He gazed at me for fully five minutes, and I did not care to break this silence. It was almost hypnotic, and for the same reason Weng did not venture to speak either.

Finally the man spoke to Weng in Chinese. It was the most unpleasant voice I have ever heard. It was not human. It was like a whisper mingled with a crow's cawing.

Was it true that I wanted a job as a bodyguard, and would I take any kind of a job, and do everything he wanted me to do under any circumstances ?

I said " Yes."

Had I ever killed a man ?

I tried to smile, and answered that perhaps I had, perhaps I had not.

Would I be afraid to kill a man?

"Not if that man made me angry, but I don't think I would ever murder in cold blood. I would kill him in self-defence, perhaps. In fact, it is more than likely that I would."

My inquisitor frowned. Then he asked me how much money I would want for killing a man in "self-defence."

Something in his expression told me that it would be more than wisdom for me to seem to put aside my scruples.

I spoke up with a boldness I did not feel:

"All the money you care to give me, a lot of food, and permission to quit the job after a certain time."

Then that terrible voice cawed again.

"Ha, ha, ha! No can quit."

I now became aware of the presence of two men I had not seen before. They were silent, heavy-faced fellows who squatted on their haunches just behind my interlocutor. I tried to peer beyond them to see if there were others. I did not want to make rash statements in the presence of too many witnesses.

Suddenly the old man dropped the subject of killing, and asked if I would be willing to go to Macao and undertake a certain job for him.

"That depends upon the job," I replied, "and, of course, upon the pay." Then I ventured to ask a personal question. I told Weng to ask what the old fellow's name was. Weng translated the question, but the man did not answer at once.

Again he covered me with one of his long stares, and his jaws moved as if he were chewing. To break this silence I repeated my question, and Weng whispered to me, "I have asked him." But he dutifully repeated the question. The man's crouching figure made an impatient sign that he *had* heard my first question, and that there was no necessity for repeating it.

Then, turning to me, he said :

" My name is — Ko Leong Tai."

Ko Leong Tai ! The dog-man !

I nodded and told him that I had heard about him ; I stretched out my hand and smiled and said that I hoped that he was all right. Then I added : " As I know who you are, I can guess what work you would ask me to do."

He looked at me as though he were rather surprised.

" Am I right," I asked him through Weng, " in stating that you have a brother in Macao who is tremendously rich, and whom you do not particularly love ? Shall I continue . . . "

Ko Leong Tai again made his impatient gesture. There was no need to continue.

" I don't think that I would care to commit murder," I added.

What did I really want ?

If he could not give me a job as a personal bodyguard I should like to be taken back in the general direction of Macao, to some village from which I could find some means of getting back to the city. I presumed that he did not care to approach too near the place.

Oh, he boasted, he did not mind the Portuguese. They did not amount to much. And what could a handful of Portuguese behind old rusty cannon do to him if he only cared to summon all of his Chinese friends ? They together could attack Macao and beat the Macanese to pulp.

I told him that I was glad he felt so strong, and that

A future West River pirate

I did not doubt his ability to do all he said. But why get into trouble? If he would kindly take me and my friends on board, and let us sail with him down the river, I would be sure to remember his kindness in some way. Maybe I could even arrange with the Portuguese to make friends with him. And again Ko Leong Tai gave me one of his appraising looks.

I remembered my state of *déshabillé* — tattered trousers, torn khaki shirt, my face unshaven, and my hands and feet very dirty. No wonder the old man had looked at me so strangely after that last remark.

Who was that girl I had with me, he asked, rather too suddenly. Was she my woman? On the spur of the moment I answered "Yes."

*　　*　　*　　*　　*

The sharp sunlight hurt my eyes when I came out of the cabin. The girl looked at me with a frightened expression, but she must have seen something reassuring in my face, for she immediately smiled happily and came towards me. Then the man who had pushed me into the cabin passed along the deck without even glancing at us. The crew resumed work—women and men—and a man brought us rifles and cartridge belts.

The little Chinese girl had probably never handled a gun. She promptly dropped the heavy military rifle on the deck, and the barrel came down on Weng's toes. He got off a string of language which must have been very bad, for the girl put her hands to her ears and fled. But one cannot flee very far on the deck of a junk, and Weng merely lifted his voice and continued to talk to her.

There was a nasty gash on his toe, and the wound bled profusely. This was the first blood we had shed during the trip, however, and I was not as sympathetic as I might have been under other circumstances. I dug into our sack which had been thrown on board, produced my shirt, tore off a sleeve, and made a bandage with which I bound his foot. Then I had the misfortune to have a yellow box of Kodak film roll out on deck.

I grabbed it up as quickly as I could and thrust it back into the sack, but too late. It had been seen.

A man came up and wanted to know what I had. He wanted to see it.

His request, however, was the result of mere curiosity. The Chinese are, perhaps, the most curious people on earth. My inquisitor was not aggressive. He asked Weng if it was candy. He had not eaten candy for many months, and he indicated that a piece would be an acceptable present. I wished that I had had some candy. That would have put an end to the incident ; but since I had none, I put my hands into the sack and opened the box, and slipped the roll of film out. Then I brought out the empty box, and showed it to the coolie. He took the carton, smelled it, licked it, and asked 'where the candy had gone. There must be some in the sack. He was in a rather jocular mood, and made a rush for the sack, emptying the whole of the contents on the deck. Out rolled ten more packages of film, not to mention my camera, and the rest of our masquerading outfit.

General commotion !

What was this ? And this ? And that ? And what was this black box ?

Half the crew gathered around us, then the others, seeing the commotion, came running to join in the excitement. Only the helmsman was left to manœuvre

the ship, and he swore loudly about the injustice that
had been done him, shouting at the men to come and
hold the helm so that he could go and take a look
also.

It was probably the best show they had had since
scuttling their last ship.

A dozen people were pointing at my camera and
shouting questions in a chorus. What was that black
box ? What did I use it for ? Did I have a devil in it ?
And a thousand other questions of similar nature. I
took the sack, and threw the clothes in, and tried to hide
the camera beneath the clothing. But too many eyes
followed the movement, and too many hands went into
the sack, and out came the camera. Rather than have
them " find out " all about it for themselves, I decided
to show it to them.

Opening the box, I pulled out the lens and loaded
the camera in full view of the whole crowd. Then I
pointed it at a couple of men, who rushed away screaming
as though they had been shot. The rest of the crew
shouted their glee.

Meantime Weng had to do a lot of explaining as to
the real nature of the camera, and grew eloquent in
his assertions that it would not hurt to have one's
picture taken. Two or three of the men had seen
photographs made in Macao, and they confirmed what
Weng said;

Then I thought that my chance had come for making
a picture of Weng. But he was too smart for me. He
turned around and said, " I takee picture you."

There was that accusing look in his eyes which made
me feel cheap. I gave the camera to him and told him
how and where to push in order to make the exposure ;

then I posted myself a short distance in front of the lens. Everybody crowded around me to see what was going to happen. They gazed at the camera, craning their necks and waiting for some kind of an explosion, perhaps fireworks. Weng took the picture, but I could see the camera swing at the moment of exposure, and knew that nothing would come of it.

The confidence of the crew had been restored. I suggested taking a picture of the women on board, and a few of the men. The women protested vociferously. No foreign devil was going to play with his magic box on them ! How did the rest of the crew know what was going to happen—if not to-day, maybe to-morrow, or next week, or next month ? But after much persuasion I finally induced them to pose, and then they rather liked it. I snapped three good pictures, but as I was preparing to take the fourth one a terrible voice screamed an order from behind me.

As the crew disappeared in all directions I turned round.

It was Ko Leong Tai. He was carried on the arms of his two retainers. His spider-like body and his horrible face were terrible to look upon in broad daylight. His head was devoid of hair, a huge flat nose spread over his face, and one tooth protruded in the middle of his mouth. He had no neck, and his monkey-like arms were flung around his carriers' shoulders.

I did some rapid thinking. I wanted to turn the camera on him and snap a picture, but intuition told me that I would be shot at once if I tried such a thing. Then he screamed once more. His left arm disengaged itself from around the neck of one of his men, and he ordered me to bring the camera to him. While I was doing so I wound up the roll of films, figuring that if he opened the camera at least the roll would be saved.

He ordered me to show the black box to him. Not to point it at him ! *Not to point it at him !* Point it toward the sea. I did as he bade me, and then I myself opened the camera. He could see now that there was nothing in it. I showed him the case, and explained how the lens works. I clicked it many times, holding my hand over the red roll of films, and finally, while moving away, I managed to get the roll out. I wetted my thumb with my tongue and fastened the gummed ribbon around the roll. My pictures were saved !

What was this, he wanted to know. I told him that I would show it to him, and told Weng to bring another roll of films as quickly as possible. I broke the box open so he could see it, and took out the new roll of film, carefully showing him how it was packed in the beautiful tin box, as all tropical films are packed.

He wanted to know what it was for, and asked if it was a new kind of cartridge to shoot with. I told him that it was only paper.

" Show me ! "

Weng stood next to me, and he handed me the new roll. I opened it, at the same time passing the exposed roll to Weng who popped it into the sack. Meantime I unrolled the whole film roll, and pointed out to Ko Leong Tai that there was no more danger in it than in any other strip of paper. He asked me to give him the white film, which was rapidly turning yellow, and I handed it to him. Then he demanded the tin box in which it had been packed. With a magnificent gesture I presented the empty box to him. He seemed pleased ; apparently he regarded it as a new toy to play with.

However, he stated that I should not play any more with this box on board the ship. Put it away! *Put it away!*

I put it away!

Then came the reaction. I lay down on my back on the deck and stared at the rushing clouds as they passed across the sun.

A little hand touched my head. My Chinese girl! Where had she been? She stroked my head until I fell asleep, mentally and physically exhausted.

*   *   *   *   *

Someone shook my shoulder violently in the midst of a dream of New York club-rooms, Fifth Avenue, and comfortable arm-chairs. A rifle was thrust into my hands.

I yawned and asked what the excitement was about.

We were going to pass a suspicious-looking junk which had been manœuvring in front of us as if trying to bar our way. The dog-man had given orders to fight our way past, if necessary. The other junk, half a cannon-shot in front of us, was a huge affair. It carried three sails and was at least half as large again as our ship. One could see that the guns had been manned, and that the crew was probably preparing to give us a broadside the moment we made an attempt to pass. Then a figure appeared on the poop and signalled to us. The dog-man must have decided that it would be better to hear the stronger man's conditions before deciding to fight; so we hove-to, dropped our anchor, and waited. Again someone shouted to us, and a man from our ship answered. Then our *sampan*, the same in which we had escaped from Fu San, was manned by two men, and they rowed over to the other ship. In a little while they returned, apparently with a message for our captain to pay up. They rowed away again, and when they returned the second time everything seemed to be all right because we immediately got up anchor and passed the big pirate. There were even friendly greetings exchanged among the members of the crew.

"Weng, find out whose ship that is," I commanded.

He went to the man who had been a messenger, and came back with the answer that it was one of Wong To Ping's guardships. As our junk had paid, and the captain had a receipt for the amount, we would not be bothered by any more guardships within Wong To Ping's territory.

So there was to be no fight after all.   I looked round. I could not help laughing, for crouching behind the mast with her gun in the most martial attitude sat the little Chinese girl, ready to blaze away at the other ship. The crew guffawed at her, and she stood up, stamping her little foot in rage, and came over to me for protection, just like a hurt child.

*   *   *   *   *

Shortly before sundown we sighted a large fleet of fishing-junks. As we approached the mouth of the river we passed a few forts on the east shore belonging to Wong To Ping. No signals were exchanged, nor did anyone molest us.

We sailed into the midst of the anchored fleet, hauled down our "canvas," and prepared to drop anchor.

These latitudes are not blessed with long twilights, but the sunsets are beautiful. The sky was aflame with all the colours of the rainbow, which gradually faded as

N

the dark purple landscape slowly sank deeper and deeper in the shadows of the coming night.

The sailors lighted torches on board all the ships, and the myriads of lights made an unreal scenic effect, such as one might dream of seeing in old Bagdad or a port of ancient India. Somewhere a drum beat a monotonous *tom! tom!* Somewhere an unseen player strummed a weird, unchanging melody on a one-string musical instrument. Somewhere I could hear the clanking of cymbals. This quiet atmosphere was occasionally disturbed, however, by the explosions of hundreds of fire-crackers, and after a while many lanterns appeared in addition to the torches. A boat moved among the junks with a man singing out the praises of his wares—a kind of spaghetti, a dish concocted of who knows what.

Then the bats came, flying low between the masts; they came in swarms of hundreds, following the clouds of insects which now swarmed above the decks. The day had been warm and the last few nights not too chilly —hence the insects, and the bats are most voracious insect-eaters.

The mosquitoes were present in uncomfortable numbers. Oh, how I wished that I were back in my soft hotel bed with a mosquito net around me. But the little girl came to my assistance. She smoked incessantly and blew the smoke in my face.

Then she fanned me with a towel.

The following morning my face was badly swollen from the mosquito bites. My hands looked like raw beef.

Weng complained that his toe felt very bad; it was the one upon which the girl had dropped the gun.

I took a look at it, and indeed it did appear ugly. The entire toe had turned blue, and he certainly was going to lose the nail. He said that he could feel the pulse beats all the way up to his knee. It was a bad sight, and blood-poisoning was the last thing I wanted to happen to him now.

Then there was a glorious sunrise, forming a real Doré picture, with streams of yellow rays bursting through the heavy clouds in all directions. Soon the orange sky turned to red, and the red to pink, and then to purple and finally to blue. Day was upon us. The drum-beating continued ; the cymbals clashed again, but now very faintly in the distance. Many of the junks hoisted sail, and one after another they moved away out toward the open sea, passing among the many islands of the delta, out of the yellow waters of the river and finally out into the blue-green of the ocean.

At last we also were ready to lift anchor, one of the last to leave the anchorage. There was another big junk preparing to leave, and as we passed it I thought I recognized the man standing next to the helmsman. I was not certain, but when we were near him I shouted. He turned and recognized me. It was Nim Tai Yeoung.

He shouted for me to come over. I told Weng to ask the captain to heave-to, so that we could leave in our dinghy, as we had been invited to board the other junk. The permission was granted to us with surprising promptness, and without losing much time in polite leave-taking, we jumped into the boat and soon wiggled our way over to the big junk, which had now hoisted its main-sail, ready to leave as soon as we had boarded her. We had all of our belongings with us, including the girl.

Our reception on Nim Tai Yeoung's junk was a marked contrast to the one that had been accorded us by our previous host. We felt that we were welcome here —camera or no camera.

There was a great show of bowing and the exchanging of polite phrases.

" May I ask you if you are on a treasure hunt ? " I inquired as soon as the formalities were over.

Nim Tai Yeoung rubbed his hands, shrugged his shoulders, and gave a smile which I interpreted to mean, " Yes, but the fact is not for publication."

We strolled aft and seated ourselves, and Nim Tai Yeoung began the conversation by asking who the pretty girl was, and if she were a special friend of mine.

I told him how she had helped me to run away from Wong Kiu.

The man looked at me. Then he spoke rapidly in pidgin-English, the substance of which follows :

" And you are still alive ? Do you know that no other stranger has ever entered Wong Kiu's village without being killed, or at least held prisoner for ransom. You actually escaped, and it did not cost you a cent ? "

" Do I look as though I had a cent ? "

" That man actually wades in blood. He loves to torture his prisoners."

I felt that this was hardly just to Wong Kiu. He had been decent to me, though he had undoubtedly killed the Russian-speaking One, and he probably kept a few prisoners which Weng had told me about. I felt moved to defend the old bandit. I started a long speech in praise of Wong Kiu, and finished by saying that probably he would never have done me any harm had I stayed longer, and that I believed the men whom he had sent to watch me were actually guarding me from possible harm.

Nim Tai Yeoung listened to me patiently, with a grave face.

" I am glad you found him so amiable."

" Have you ever met him ? " I went on challengingly.

" No," he said, " I never have, but two of my sons have."

" Well ? " I continued.

" They both died by his hand."

There was nothing I could say. For a long time I remained silent, and then I stole a look at Nim Tai Yeoung.

" It was a long time ago," he continued, " but we Chinese never forget such things. One day perhaps I will kill him, or then again he perhaps will kill me. Who knows ? "

* * * * *

We were sailing southward with a good wind. We passed island after island, and Nim Tai Yeoung told me their names as we sailed by them. There was the large Tiger Island, the Tai Fu, and south of it the second and third Tiger Islands. Beyond them to the south-east was the White Forest Water, and south of this again the San Hoi Chauck, which is literally " Where Three Seas Join."

" How far are we going to sail ? " I asked. " Where is your treasure island ? "

" Beyond Seaman's Island," Nim Tai Yeoung answered. " Somewhere to the east. Wait and see."

He had the cook kill three chickens and fry them for my benefit, in white man's fashion, as he called it.

About two o'clock he went below, and asked if I

cared to join him in a pipe of opium. The wind had turned completely, and we were tacking for a couple of hours on each leg. As I did not care for opium, there was nothing for me to do but lie down on the deck and listen to the waves beating against the ship's sides and the creaking of the tackle overhead, and to follow the flight of the seagulls as they wheeled about our masts.

It was good to be again among people whom I felt I could trust. True, I did not know them very well, but the crew were a friendly lot who grinned and tried to talk to me. The little Cantonese I spoke did not help at all, for they spoke a good Chinese Hakka, or some other South China dialect. Yet I had a certain sense of security ; I knew that I could slumber and wake up alive.

*   *   *   *   *

As I lay there on the deck, half-dozing, my thoughts turned to Wong Kiu. I remembered what my missionary friend had first told me of Wong Kiu. He had described him as a middle-aged, gentle, well-dressed Chinese. How different I had found him. He was well dressed to be sure, as Chinese rigging goes, but he certainly was not gentle. There must have been some reason why Wong Kiu had made this totally different impression on my friend the clergyman, but I could not figure out that reason. The gentle " sky-pilot " had also told me that Wong To Ping, the second " big stick " in this neighbourhood, was a man of terrifying appearance, a rustic and a ruffian, smelling of opium, using vile language, killing prisoners for fun, and eating their hearts and livers to acquire their strength. If Wong Kiu had impressed him as a gentleman, what should I expect of Wong To Ping, if I ever met him ?

Suddenly two armoured junks came sailing out from behind the San Hoi Chauck and headed towards us.

Commotion began immediately. Someone ran down to fetch Nim Tai Yeoung, and he came on deck, pale and feverish under the influence of the " happy smoke."

" What is up ? " I asked.

" No savee—maybe pirates, maybe not."

" What pirates ? Wong To Ping ? "

" Maybe."

It seemed rather strange to be on a junk pursued by pirates. It had been the other way before, when I had sailed with pirates and we had caught up with trading junks, and had made them " pay up " or go to Davy Jones's locker.

The crew jabbered excitedly and ran back and forth on deck purposelessly, pointing at the two ships and shouting. One already had crossed our path and was now sailing parallel to us ; the one on the other side followed us, gradually drawing nearer.

The larger of the two junks sent a shot across our bows, a signal for us to stop. A boat came over with five men on board. A man, apparently the leader, stood in the bow. He was fifty or fifty-five years old, a big, husky fellow. He wore a belt with a pistol, and the others wore cartridge belts and carried rifles.

As soon as he had climbed on board this man came straight up to me, apparently thinking that I was the captain or owner. He was greatly excited, and fired question after question at me, so rapidly that Weng had no time to translate. Finally, I motioned for the man to stop until Weng could tell me what he wanted.

Was I a Government official or a Customs man ?

What was I doing in these waters ?   What cargo did we carry ?   Was I making maps and trying to find harbours for Customs boats ?

I did not like his manner.   He played entirely too much with the pistol in his belt.   What right had he to stop me ?   I asked him through Weng.   The fellow seemed to be flabbergasted.   What right had he to stop us indeed !   He laughed out loudly, but grew red with anger.

Yes, what right had he to stop me ?   If he would come down and talk matters over with my friend, Nim Tai Yeoung, perhaps he would be able to calm himself over a cup of tea.   Nim Tai Yeoung heard Weng translate this, and sneaked down into the cabin.   I understood that he had gone to arrange for the tea, but I went on with my bluff.

If my friend Wong Kiu ever found out . . .

I never got any further.   As soon as I had mentioned Wong Kiu's name this murderous-looking chap looked at me in surprise and asked Weng what I knew about Wong Kiu.   Weng dutifully translated my statement that we had just been his guests, had visited him for some days, and were now peacefully on our way back to Macao.

The bandit stared at me in astonishment ; then all five of them talked excitedly for a few minutes.

What had I done at Wong Kiu's place, he wanted to know.

I replied that I had offered him my friendship and my services together with the services of Weng and of my Russian friends.

" What services ? " he demanded.

" Well," I said, " I am not going to talk about this

matter on deck, but if you care to come down into the cabin I'll be glad to talk things over."

Leaving his four men on deck, he descended into the cabin, where Nim Tai Yeoung was awaiting us. Four cups of tea were on the table ; the fourth was for Weng.

I described myself as an ambassador from a number of Russians who wanted work, and were desperate with hunger. We were willing to join anybody who would pay us, I said, and to protect our employers with our lives if necessary.

How many were we ?

Oh, many, many. The reason I had come was to take a " look-see," and if anything could be arranged, I would return to Macao and send word to my friends. They would join me wherever our employer wished us to go.

In the dim light of the cabin I could see that the idea struck the pirate favourably.

What had Wong Kiu said ?

Oh, Wong Kiu had not been big enough for us after all. He could not pay us what we wanted. He had wanted us badly, I said, but I had flatly refused his offer.

My interrogator began to show signs of interest. He wanted to know if I would be willing to talk the matter over with him, and would I like to join him ?

I told him it would depend upon who he was. If he was a big enough man I would be glad to make any arrangements. What was his name ?

Oh, he said, people called him Wong To Ping.

Yes, I would be glad to talk things over.

Would I be " kind enough " to come to his village ?

Which village ?

Lai Chi San.

I would be glad to, I said, provided he made himself responsible for the safety of my companions and myself.

Who were my companions? He pointed to Weng and then toward the girl. Turning to Nim Tai Yeoung, I begged him to take her with him to Macao, to which he acquiesced. I felt greatly relieved. So it was arranged that Weng and I should board Wong To Ping's junk and return with him to his haunts.

Soon the two Chinese were talking amiably, bowing politely to each other, and each one shaking his own hands as an expression of respect. I believe that Nim Tai Yeoung was very grateful to me for saving him from being pirated.

I told Weng to see the girl and tell her that she could go back to Macao now, but when he delivered the message an astonishing thing happened. She did not want to go to Macao; she wanted to go with us in Wong To Ping's boat. Two men had to hold her back, and the last thing I heard were her screams: "Save life! Save life!"

Poor little girl!

PART SEVEN

WE were met with curiosity on board Wong To Ping's little ship.

It was not a large junk, but very swift, and everything on board her was spick and span. She carried two modern breech-loading cannons besides the usual collection of ancient muzzle-loaders. The two modern guns were well oiled and brightly polished.

I turned round and took a last look at Nim Tai Yeoung's ship. It swung gracefully in the wind, and I could see the little woman standing alone, gazing in our direction. I waved to her, and she waved back. Then I followed Wong To Ping into his cabin.

The outcome of our discussion was that if I found things satisfactory after having visited his village I would return to Macao and bring back my " White Army."

How many were we ?

Oh, up to one hundred men, I lied.

That was excellent, he said. All well trained in the use of arms ?

Of course.

And could my men make soldiers out of his men ?

They certainly could. That was exactly what they had been doing before they were turned out by the Nationalists.

Wong To Ping was now highly excited. He could not do enough to please me. We sat in his cabin and drank the usual tea. There were some sweet cookies, too, but they were entirely too sweet for me.

He thought it an excellent idea, this addition of the Russians to his forces. He would treat us like his own sons, he said. We could have our own houses, and he would supply as many women as we wanted. He would give us chow—rice, pigs, sheep and chickens.

"How about pay?" I asked. "These things are all well enough, but we will have to have cold cash besides."

He assured me that he had money enough.

"In that case," I replied, "I and my comrades will make you the strongest man in this part of the country. Not Wong Kiu or Lai Choi San or any other independent 'princeling' will ever question your superiority."

But here Wong To Ping began to hesitate. How was he to be sure what I had said was the truth. I gave him a hard look and did not deign to answer. I indicated that I was hurt to the depths of my soul. Rising, I bowed politely, and said that I wanted to go back to Macao as soon as possible.

The bluff worked. Wong To Ping hurried to apologize. He assured me that he had never meant to question my integrity. He was just being careful. He looked round the luxurious cabin, and said: "You are my friend; anything you wish is yours. I am your friend. If there is anything you wish done, all of my men are at your service."

At this I bowed and peace was restored. We sipped our tea, and I tried to swallow another cookie. The ship careened to starboard, and I noticed a very antique European watch hanging on the wall. It was a beautiful watch, at least three inches in diameter, the dial surrounded with pearls and red stones. A second hand was ticking, and once when the ship careened more than usual the watch swung sidewise, and I saw that the back of the case was beautifully painted, and the name of the painting dated from the latter part of the seventeenth century. Wong To Ping followed my gaze and asked : " You likee watch ? "

I told Weng to tell him that I liked it very much indeed. It was a beautiful thing.

" Oh, this is no good—too old. Next time you go to Macao you can bring me a new one. I give you this. The pearls no good, and red stones no good too. You have the watch ? "

I certainly would " likee have the watch," I thought, but I politely refused. However, the more strenuously I refused the more he urged me to take it.

Finally, I accepted it with profuse thanks. I immediately opened the case. It looked as though it had been made yesterday, so highly polished was it. I smelt it. It did not smell like brass or bronze. Perhaps it was gold. There was something engraved within. " Timothy Y. Williamson, London," I read. Timothy Y. Williamson ! I remembered something about this watchmaker; he had lived towards the latter part of the seventeenth century. The watch had probably never been repaired. It was a wonderful gift indeed. I counted the pearls—there were forty-four. I counted the red stones—rubies or garnets, I did not know which —there were also forty-four.*

This gift required a return present from me, and what should I give ? I prayed that he would not ask for my camera, and then I searched in my pocket, and for want

* I still have the watch. A London dealer recently appraised it at forty pounds. (See photograph facing page 244.)

of anything better to give him I handed over my cheap
Ingersoll with a polite bow.

" It isn't as good as yours," I told Weng to say to
Wong To Ping; " but it is a good watch, and I have
brought it all the way from America."

He took it, listened to the works, and without a
word hung it in the place where the old watch had been.
It was evident that he was pleased to own an American
watch. He asked me how long I had had it, and I told
him that I had bought it about a year ago.

Then somebody came and reported that we were
nearing land. We went up on deck.

Wong To Ping told me that as soon as we landed
he would send for a tailor and have suits made for me.
The way we looked now—well, we were a disgrace. Wong
To Ping would not have his honoured guests walk about
barefoot and in torn shirts and trousers. As a matter of
fact, he discussed at considerable length the kind of suit
I desired. Would I like to have a Chinese suit, with
skirt and jacket? His men would provide us with
whatever we needed. And we could live with him or
separately as we desired.

We suggested that we should live with him.

*   *   *   *   *

Several years ago a remarkable piracy was carried out
right in the middle of Hong-Kong harbour. A ferry on
the run from Victoria to Yaumati was held up in the
middle of the bay by a band of pirates. The helmsman
felt the cold muzzle of a pistol against his head, and
was commanded to turn the ship around in the general
direction of Macao. Meantime the rest of the band kept
the passengers covered, took all their money and

jewels, and landed them somewhere outside Hong-Kong, while the ferry proceeded to a rendezvous somewhere on the West River. Wong To Ping was the man who had headed this expedition. He had thought that a ferry would be a good addition to his list of trophies. So he decided to acquire one, a municipal ferry at that, but he had forgotten that it would require coal to burn and oil to keep the engine from getting hot. The engineer told him that this would be his trouble, and somehow managed to persuade the pirate chief to release the boat as soon as the gang had landed.

Weng related the whole story to him, and I asked if it were true. There was a merry look in his eyes, and his body shook with laughter. He remembered the expedition well, and admitted that part of the story was true. He had pirated the Yaumati ferry all right.

* * * * *

Late at night we sailed back into the waters of the West River to the place where I had boarded Nim Tai Yeoung's junk. Wong To Ping was squatting on a cannon, not unlike a monkey on a tree trunk, gazing in the direction of a big anchored junk without masts, which was hidden behind a small peninsula at our right.

" What is that ? " I asked Wong To Ping, and Weng translated his " never mind."

The ship looked very much like a floating prison. There was an armed guard padding back and forth along the deck.

" Say," I said, trying to be jocular, " is this the place where you keep your prisoners ? "

" Who told you that ! "

I smiled innocently. " Why, Wong Kiu, of course."

He burst out into a flood of purest Chinese profanity. Evidently he believed my story.

Wong To Ping turned abruptly to me, and said: " Want to see ? "

I admitted that I would be tickled to death, but when I saw the gleam in his eye I added that of course he should guarantee that I would come out again. Wong To Ping thought that was a good joke and began to laugh. We were getting along wonderfully.

He turned to Weng, and said that during my stay he did not want us to take any pictures of his place. He knew very well what a camera was. He had been in Hong-Kong and Shanghai, and had even had a few photographs taken of himself.

" Where ? " I interrupted.

" Never mind ! " he replied.

" Was it in the Hong-Kong prison ? "

He laughed outright. I must have hit the nail on the head, but how he had come out without being hanged is beyond my comprehension.

" What were you in for, Wong To Ping ? "

" Never mind."

" Look here, I have been in there myself. I can tell you all about it. Did you ever carry shot and stone ? Did you ever pick oakum ? And how many hangings did you see ? "

I continued without mercy and, laughing, he motioned me to keep quiet. Doubtless those were rather sad memories for him. I wondered if the old man had ever been flogged.

" Why don't you want me to take pictures, Wong To Ping ? I'd like a picture of yourself, and the house where you live, and your village, and perhaps a boat or two. I want to show my friends when I go back that I have actually been in your house as an honoured guest " (I emphasized the "honoured guest"), " and assure them that if they were to follow me back to your village they would receive the same treatment. I should be proud to tell them what a fine man my friend Wong To Ping is."

" Yes," he mocked, speaking through Weng, " and when somebody gets hold of the pictures of myself, and my house, and my friends, and the junks, and then some policeman in Hong-Kong meets some of these friends on the street that will be the last of the friends."

I did not argue the question.

" Let me have the camera," he suggested, " and when you go away I 'll give it back again."

"Wong To Ping," I replied, " you can go to hell! I'll not let that camera out of my hands. However, I'll promise not to take a single picture."

He asked if I would surely abide by my promise, and I answered that I would.

Did I swear by my children ?

Not only by my children, I assured him, but also by all my ancestors, and if he had a white rooster he could kill it right then and there and I would swear by its blood. That was enough for the old man. He seemed satisfied.

*   *   *   *   *

Night descended. We were all to sleep on board and not to go ashore. The ghost-like form of another ship floated in out of the darkness and hove to. The anchor splashed in the water, and somebody shouted. Then all was quiet around us. I opened the hatch leading to Wong To Ping's cabin, and was invited to come down.

o

I was glad to get below, as the night was getting cold and my "uniform" was very scanty. Weng was there already, enjoying a steaming bowl of rice and drinking rice wine. I was soon following his example. The rice tasted wonderful, and the wine was more than a welcome addition to the meal. We all grew happy, and I was soon thinking that the world was a fine place to live in after all.

Weng and I had been shown to a bunk separated by a thin partition from the one Wong To Ping was occupying. The ventilation was not of the best, as the hatch was kept hermetically closed, and Wong To Ping's tobacco was extremely strong. I was glad that the old man had not chosen this time for a drag of opium. He and one of his men played a game of checkers or some other game while leisurely reclining on their bunks, occasionally removing their pipes long enough to discuss further ventures or the business at hand.

Weng leaned over and whispered to me that he had heard somebody among the crew say that in the village where we were going there was one Chinese who spoke Russian and another who spoke English. There was also a girl who had gone to school in America. . . .

"That sounds interesting," I interrupted. "What school?"

He could not say, but he would try to find out.

What a chance of a lifetime for a newspaper man! If I could only get hold of the co-ed, what a write-up it would make! I told Weng that he would certainly have to find out all about this girl; moreover, he should see to it that I had my camera with me when we met her.

"Camera?" He looked dumbfounded.

"Yes, camera."

" Oh, camera, that is all gone," and he pointed to the partition behind which Wong To Ping was amusing himself in conversation with his friend. " The Chinaman say you no wantee camera no more."

" *Oh, hell !* "

Somehow I refrained from jumping up and rushing to Wong To Ping and demanding my camera. Probably it would have been " not proper fashion." After all, I was in the old man's clutches, and should be grateful that I was being treated the way I was—as the honoured guest.

*   *   *   *   *

We left the junk at daylight. Four more junks had arrived during the night, and about twenty-five of those long, highly-polished war canoes. This was apparently his " naval base." There was also a fort with high walls and two muzzle-loading cannon, to control the traffic on the river.

Wong To Ping led the way into the bush. For several miles we struggled along a narrow path, winding up and down the hills and past small villages of bamboo huts, swarming with the usual multitude of poultry and pigs. About a hundred men, most of them members of the junk's crews, followed us in Indian file, and each carried a rifle in addition to multitudinous bundles. I noticed one group of prisoners, with hands bound behind their backs and with nooses round their necks. The neck ropes were connected with the hands of the men following, so that the slightest movement would draw the noose tight.

" Why don't you leave them on the boat, Wong To Ping ? " I asked him. By this time I had forgotten about the camera.

He explained that he was going to have a "talkie-talkie" with them before "putting them away."

What did he mean to do with them? I asked. Kill them or keep them prisoners on board the ship? From his sly answer I gathered that this was a matter that depended upon the possibilities of making a decent profit by keeping them.

"And if it is not profitable, what then?"

"Hens that do not lay eggs are not worth their keep."

I took a look at the flea-bitten bunch of prisoners and decided that there were some among them who stood small chance of being retained.

"By the way, Wong To Ping," I finally blurted out, "where is my camera?"

He stopped, and the long train behind me had to stop too. He button-holed Weng, and his face wore a positive expression which could be translated only into: "Look here, my friend, let this be the last time I hear anything about the subject."

Weng translated it as: "Tell the foreigner that I wish to remain friends with him."

*   *   *   *   *

Weary and foot-sore, with Weng limping very badly, his foot bound up in filthy rags, we finally arrived at Wong To Ping's own village. It was not a large place, but larger than Fu San. It was richer looking, the houses were better, and there were even a couple of temples and joss-houses.

The men camped in the first big courtyard, and Wong To Ping invited us to follow him. Half-way through the yard he stopped and again faced Weng with the same half-threatening look that he had favoured him with before when I had asked for my camera. When he had finished talking I asked Weng what it was all about.

" You told him you Russian. He going to find. If not true, no much good."

I wondered what devilry the old murderer had in mind. Soon he came out with two men, one of whom was a smiling, bald-headed, oily-looking old bandit. This man came straight up to me bowing and smiling a Uriah Heep smile ; then he addressed me in the worst Russian I have ever heard. I asked him in Russian to repeat what he had said, and he did so. Still his jargon was unintelligible.

I saw Wong To Ping's face darken, but I refused to be beaten. I spluttered away for a minute or two, ridiculing the man for not knowing better Russian. I knew that I had overwhelmed him by my knowledge of the language, and Wong To Ping and his other companion showed that they were impressed. Then, turning to Weng, I told him to tell Wong To Ping not to bring any more people to me who spoke only *coolie* Russian, and who had probably been servants to a servant of a servant to some low-class Russian soldier. Wong To Ping himself should have known better, he who was so just. I went on praising him for a while in order to get the old smile into his face.

It worked. Wong To Ping jerked his thumb, and the linguist disappeared. Whether or not it was for punishment I do not know, but the fellow was later assigned to us as a house-boy.

Weng had apparently taken a dislike to him, probably because this was the first time that he, a servant, had ever had a servant at his disposal. He almost rushed the poor man to death. Nothing was ever good enough for Weng. The water was either too cold or too hot, the food was bad, and the dishes too dirty, or the tea was not brewed right. I've never seen anyone take such delight in making another's life miserable as Weng did while this wretched creature was our servant.

*   *   *   *   *

Wong To Ping brought a native Chinese doctor to "look-see" Weng's foot. It was badly swollen and showed signs of blood-poisoning. The boy complained that he was feverish. I told him to keep away from the Chinese doctor, who would probably feed him with pulverized dragon teeth and monkey paws; but Weng professed absolute belief in Chinese medicine men.

An old man came to see us late in the afternoon, and in his dirty rags were actually dried monkey hands, pulverized snakes, chicken embryos in a bottle, not to mention an ointment made of cockroaches and beetles.

I retired.

Poor Weng was in very bad shape. Unless something was done about his foot he stood in a fair way to lose it. I walked out in the courtyard and sat down on the steps which led up to the platform. In a nearby room four Chinese, Wong To Ping's Number One men, I presumed, were playing mah-jongg, and in contrast to most Chinese games, this was a silent, serious one. The stakes must have been high. Each player lifted the tiles with such an expression as a man might assume if his head depended upon the turn of a lucky number.

In front of me a centipede was crawling leisurely across the path. It was a beautiful insect with a black, shiny body and red feet. Another centipede came scrambling over from the other side, and then they met.

I don't know whether what followed was a fight or a love scene, but it went on with terrible intensity for a few minutes.

Somebody approached me from the back. Somehow the last weeks had made me very jumpy. Footsteps in the dark, whispering voices and the company of pirates, professional murderers and robbers had not been soothing to my nerves.

A servant brought me a pair of slippers. And how good they felt on my feet! He also fetched a pair of trousers and a silk jacket, which I promised myself never to return to Wong To Ping. It was a glorious satin thing, black with a flowery design woven into the materials.

I lacked only one thing—a good hot bath.

I got my bath.

I asked for hot water, towels, and a piece of soap, and went to the backyard. The pirates did not understand what I meant by soap; probably they never had used any in their lives. But the water was hot, and shamelessly I undressed, and stood stark naked while I scrubbed my body with hot towels until I glowed like a spanked baby.

Then I heard snickering around me. I looked up, and in every door and in every window, I believe even on the roofs, there were onlookers. They must have admired the spectacle I presented.

I wanted to cover myself with a towel, but blast it all! somebody had taken it away.

I felt physically new-born. My body was clean, or at least much cleaner than it had been for many days, and so were my clothes. What would not I have given for a nice soft bed.

In one of the many courtyards I saw friend " doctor " trying to sneak out of the house with his bundle. I swooped down upon him and asked him in my best Chinese how Weng was. The " doctor " did not understand me, at least he pretended that he did not ; so I grabbed him by the arm and marched him off to our room.

Weng was prostrated, pale-faced, and apparently unconscious. His foot had been covered with some kind of muddy paste that made it look hideous. I started to examine the foot, but the " doctor " tackled me. He shoo'd and sizzled and spat and behaved like a wild cat, trying to save the result of his labours, and then Weng opened his eyes.

He stared at me, and finally asked what was the matter.

" How do you feel, Weng ? "

" Not good, but my foot no pain."

By dark Weng was up and around. He said that his foot was all right now. I could not very well accuse him of being a liar, as the foot was his and not mine, and so was the pain. I wished, however, that I could have been present when the " doctor " had put him through this " horse-cure." I might have learned something.

*   *   *   *   *

Later in the evening Wong To Ping's Russian-speaking servant came in. He bowed and bowed and bowed again. I asked him in Russian what he had on his mind, and finally I understood that he wanted me to do him a favour. I told him that I would be glad to oblige him if I could.

Well . . . it was this way . . . he really did not

know how to express himself, but . . . well, he really did not know very much Russian . . . and would I please not give him away?

How could I do that?

Oh, by telling Wong To Ping that he knew Russian very well indeed.

"Of course, you know a little bit," I said, "but do you really understand what I am saying to you?"

"Oh, yes, yes, yes!"

"Well," I taunted, "your knowledge is greater than I thought."

It developed that all he wanted me to do was to nod and say "yes, yes," whenever he addressed me. This was to be done, of course, when Wong To Ping was present.

After all, it was a small matter. Why not help the poor devil if I could? I told him I would do it.

The room in which we slept was very neat and clean. The windows had no glass in them; they were covered with heavy rice paper. Occasionally when somebody wanted to peep into the room a finger would be put through the paper. Once I caught a finger coming through the window, held it for a while, with the owner squealing. Weng laughed until he almost shook the paste off his foot.

"Bite it!" he suggested.

*   *   *   *   *

In the morning Weng again had a very bad pain in his foot. The toe was swollen, and I suggested that I should lance it. He said that he would be willing to let me do anything I wanted to do if I could only promise him relief.

" Let us call the boy and get a sharp knife. And tell him to boil it."

In spite of his pain, Weng laughed.

" Why boil knife ?   Boil eggs and chicken, but knives no good boiled."

We got a knife, and I went with the boy to the kitchen, a huge establishment wherein at least ten persons were always at work cooking. The place was full of flies and cats. The food was being mixed with dirty hands, and water was not used abundantly for washing purposes. But we got hold of a kettle into which I poured some water, and I boiled the knife for a good ten minutes. Then I lifted it out with a spoon, and holding it by the handle, marched up to the room. I wished for some sterilized gauze and absorbent cotton, but neither was to be had. The moment I made the incision the " doctor " came hopping into the room. The devil must have sent him. He began to yell like a maniac ; so I kicked him out and returned to the operation.

Throughout the day I did not see Wong To Ping at all, but in the evening he sent a message that he was going to sail away, and asked if I wanted to go with him.

" Yes," I replied, " I should like to very much, but unfortunately my partner, Weng, is ill and cannot move, and as I do not speak Chinese well enough to be understood I am lost without his help."

The messenger went away, but came back with another man, who explained to me in reasonably good pidgin-English that he knew English very well, and that Wong To Ping was anxious to have me go with him. I told him that I would be glad to go.

By daybreak next morning I was ready and waiting for somebody to call for me and take me to Wong To Ping's " picnic." A little boy, not more than eight years old, came to our part of the house and shouted for the " foreign devil." I appreciated Wong To Ping's consideration in sending this boy. What a vast difference from Wong Kiu. When he had wanted me fetched he had sent half an army. So this " foreign devil" grabbed the astonished boy by the hand and told him to lead on. Mightily pleased, he walked by my side through many courtyards into the " office" of the great chief. I will never forget this boy. He seemed to be a bright little chap, and very important he looked when he delivered his prisoner into the hands of the old murderer.

Wong To Ping greeted me in a friendly manner. The English-speaking Chinese, dressed in a grey skirt with a blue jacket and a skull cap, was also there, and bowed politely. Tea was brought in. This act is only a polite gesture towards an honoured guest. As often as not one does not drink it at all, but as the morning was cold I poured out a cup and drank it. It was the strongest green tea I had ever tasted.

Then we were all ready—a group of about forty men, most of whom were armed—and we marched down to the river. A fleet of *sampans* carried us to Wong To Ping's junk, the same one which had brought me to his domains.

I asked where we were going.

"Wong To Ping wants you to do him a favour," the interpreter told me.

Then the pirate revealed his wishes. He had brought along the camera and all the other paraphernalia with him. There was one certain place he wanted to have photographed. I told him that I would certainly be glad

to oblige him. And then he wanted this picture, the man
continued ; he wanted to send it to Wong Kiu.

" To Wong Kiu ? "

" Yes, to Wong Kiu. Wong Kiu has been meddling
into Wong To Ping's business lately, and the result has
not been good for Wong Kiu. Many of his junks have
been taken away and many men are prisoners in Wong
To Ping's hands. Messengers have been sent to Wong
Kiu with letters from the imprisoned men, but Wong Kiu
always replies that he does not believe those letters. His
brave men would never let themselves be taken prisoners."

So Wong To Ping's idea was that I should furnish
" Exhibit A " as proof, and take a photograph of these
prisoners. I was only too eager to use my camera again.
I admit that I planned to double-cross him. If only
I could get the camera loaded with a new roll of
six films, I was certain that I could get a picture of the
old man himself. If only I could lay hands on that
camera !

*   *   *   *   *

It was a cold day. An icy wind blew from the north,
and all the sailors had put on their heavy coats. I
was half-frozen and shivering, and Wong To Ping sent
me his heavy ulster.

We had set sail, accompanied by two auxiliary junks.
Fire-crackers were burned, drums were beaten, and the
gods must surely have been appeased by all the noise
that was made. We sailed at least three hours, came out
to the open sea, luffed westward, and approached a tiny
island guarded by two junks sailing back and forth near
the shore. At a distance it looked as though the island
was covered with sheep, but when we came nearer

we could see that these were crowds of human beings, covering the whole island. There were at least two hundred people—men, women, and children—all of them prisoners taken by Wong To Ping in " honest warfare " against his rival and compatriot Wong Kiu.

The two other junks had come to relieve the guardships, and also to bring fresh food to the prisoners.

No wonder Wong To Ping was anxious to get rid of this crowd. Wong Kiu must have known, too, that he would not murder them—there were too many. Of course, they were uncomfortable and hungry, as the food was certainly too scantily apportioned, but that was a small matter in China, where hardships are taken for granted. We landed and, surrounded by a bodyguard of twelve men, marched ashore. Loud curses were shouted at us. Some of the women yelled hysterically, and one old man fell down on his knees crying bitterly. For some reason they addressed their supplications to me. Perhaps they thought I was their saviour, a Government official from Macao or Hong-Kong. If they had only known !

While I was standing in the midst of this group a man came to me and handed me my camera and *one package of films*. I obediently opened the camera, put in the film and got a good view. As soon as I had taken the picture the same man came up and demanded the camera from me. There was no chance for me to protest, but I would have given anything to have had the camera just by myself for five minutes or so.

As I handed the camera back to the man Wong To Ping wanted to know how soon he could have the picture.

I replied that I would give him one as soon as I developed the film and made a print.

Wong To Ping looked at me curiously. How long would that take?

It all depended upon how soon I could return to Macao.

To Macao?

Certainly, I could not develop any pictures here. I tried to explain that I had no dark room or chemicals, but it was easy to see that Wong To Ping did not believe me. He was certain that for some unknown reason I was delaying the delivery of the picture.

There was an angry look in his eyes. Silently he turned round, marched down to the beach, leaving the shouting, clamouring crowd behind him. We boarded the junk and sailed back to the " fort." He did not speak a single word to me during the whole trip, and once back in the village we parted without formalities.

Weng had got hold of his Chinese " doctor " while I was away, and once more he boasted that there was no pain in the foot. The " doctor " had said graciously that it was a good thing I had " bled " the foot. And indeed it did look better. During the night Weng woke me up to inform me that there was still no pain, and in the morning he insisted upon hopping around. His injury was healing and from then on he would not permit either the " doctor " or me to get near his sore toe. Apparently he did not appreciate our services.

*   *   *   *   *

Nothing happened the next day, but on the day following Wong To Ping appeared in person. He said he wanted to know all about the picture and the camera.

Then through Weng I tried to explain the process of photography, and how the film is sensitive to daylight, and why one must have a dark room with a red light and chemicals. I told him that if he could arrange for me to go to Macao I could promise to have the picture back within a few hours. This time he really believed me; he said he would think it over and decide how to send me to Macao.

He seemed pleased at the prospect of getting the picture, and said that he would try to arrange matters so that I could sail within a few days. Then he suddenly faced me and demanded how he could be sure that I would return. I smiled at him. *I* was not anxious to go to Macao, I said. What I wanted was to get a job for myself and my friends. Moreover, I pointed out that here was an excellent chance for me to bring a few of them back with me. Wong To Ping nodded thoughtfully; then he suggested that I should go with him to another part of the building and talk things over.

Weng went with us; he was hopping about with the help of two sticks, and he gave me a sign that he had a message for me. I went over to him.

What was it?

Did I remember the English-speaking girl who had been educated in America?

"Yes," I replied.

"She no more."

"What do you mean? Is she dead?"

"No, she not dead. She go Canton, melly big General, and now live in Nanking."

He also told me that some of Wong To Ping's men wanted him to become a member of their "tong." He had replied that he would not think of it unless I became a member also.

Good boy! There was a novel idea!

I sat down in Wong To Ping's guest-room on one of his carved blackwood chairs. All the furniture was of blackwood. The floor was of red brick. In one corner of the room some kind of compass hung suspended on a thread from the ceiling. It was a queer-looking, square board with Chinese characters inscribed all around the needle.

" What is this ? " I queried.

Wong To Ping answered: " This is the thing which tells my luck—whether it is good or bad. When you came here several days ago the needle told me my luck was good."

I looked at him surprised.

" Well," I hesitated, " suppose the needle had told you that your luck was bad ? "

" Then your luck would have been very bad too."

Thus things depend on small matters. I am sure that my life had been at that time dependent upon the point of a needle, and that is indeed a fairly small space to hang your fate on.

He clapped his hands and told the servant, as I found out later from Weng, to go through the adjoining rooms and see if anyone was listening to us.

" I am going to ask you to do something for me," he said, " and I am going to pay you well for doing it."

" Stop right there ! " I interrupted. " If it is murdering or killing a man in self-defence, then count me out. Not so many days ago somebody else asked me to do that very thing, and I refused."

" No, I want you to take something with you when you go to Macao."

Well, that was entirely another matter.

But it was something very valuable.   Could he depend upon me ?

That was entirely up to him, I said.   Was it jewellery or money ?

" Money," he answered.

In that case, I said, I would like him to send somebody with me.   This neighbourhood was not any too secure, and " accidents " could happen.

Yes, he agreed.   Perhaps it would be a good idea to send a couple of men along.

*   *   *   *   *

I asked Weng to tell me more about the clan he had been invited to join.   He said it was a secret society, but he was not certain as to its exact nature.   One man had vaguely mentioned something about ceremonies, oaths to be taken, white roosters to be killed, and the passing of guardians at the gates.   That sounded very much like a regular secret society initiation ; I was very much interested.

" By the way," I said the next time I saw Wong To Ping, " why not have Weng and me join your society ? "

" What society ?   What do you know about it ? "

I tried to look innocent.

" Oh, nothing, nothing.   I just thought that . . . Wong To Ping, you want me to become one of your men, and bring hundreds of my friends along.   You are entrusting me with money, and you have been kind enough to let me walk round your village.   You have shown me your prison junk.   You have asked me to keep this secret, and now you even want me to go to Macao and take your money with me.   How do you

P

know that I won't tell everybody what I have seen here ? "

Wong To Ping did not reply immediately. When he did speak, it was to utter an enigma.

" To break the law of the Hall is death ; to follow the law of the Hall is death."

It sounded interesting, but it looked to me very much like a one-sided proposition. Whichever way you turned the result was just the same—death !

But it was intriguing.

The old murderer must have thought better of my suggestion, for Weng got word that something was going to happen. The whole of the next day we could see groups of men standing and talking, and occasionally pointing at us and grinning when they thought themselves unobserved. On the following morning we were given no breakfast, and when Weng complained to one of the cooks, the man rushed back to the kitchen as if to fetch the order, and Weng came back and said, " Chow bye'n bye." But no chow came.

By noon I was very hungry. I decided to go to the kitchen on my own account and try to get some fish and a bowl of rice, but I was stopped by one of the numerous cooks and shoved out through the door. However, his manner was not unfriendly.

" Bye'n bye," he promised.

Weng looked disappointed. He had more news for me. We were not going to have anything to eat for the whole day, and only rice wine to drink. The wine made me dizzy all day long.

About six in the afternoon Weng and I went strolling through the courtyards.

I heard two excited voices on the other side of the wall.

It sounded as though an angry man was asking questions, or accusing somebody of something. We loitered along where we could hear it, but before long a man came into the courtyard, and when he saw us he told us to get out of the yard. A whiff of opium fumes reached us from a half-closed door, and then I heard a scream from the other side. I stopped instantly. It had sounded very much like the shriek of a woman, but the accusing voice continued its harangue. As we were hurried out of the yard through a circular gate in the wall I heard the scream a second time. I stopped again. This time I was pushed roughly, and the gate was shut from the inside. Yet I could hear that terribly accusing voice now as a faint murmur, until it finally died away. There were no more screams.

There was a lotus pond in a nearby garden with large green leaves floating on the quiet surface of the water and also some beautiful flowers arranged so as to form the Chinese character for Happiness. A big grey bird was singing a strange melody in the sunshine, and then I heard the throbbing, heavy sound from a temple gong a long way off.

*   *   *   *   *

Weng and I were now more than hungry ; we were famished.

"Let's go out of the house, if we can," I said, " and buy some food."

Weng looked as though he did not approve of the proposition. Still, he was hungry, and reason breaks down before the demands of a hungry stomach. Our heads were whirling from the rice wine we had drunk, and somewhat unsteadily we made our way towards the gate, but a guard stopped us. Our foraging expedition was apparently doomed to be a failure.

We returned to our room and I stretched out upon the floor. After a time I dropped off to sleep. When I awakened, it was almost dark. Weng was sitting in a corner with two steaming bowls in front of him, shovelling rice into his mouth with both hands, without troubling to use a spoon or chopsticks. There was some rice, a bottle of rice wine, and a pot of tea beside me, but I no longer felt hungry. I had a violent headache. I drank some tea, and that seemed to relieve the pain..

Somebody had brought a jar of incense sticks, and the faint glow of their smouldering tips was the only illumination of the room. I reflected that we were probably being purified. Then somebody struck a big gong beneath our window. The suddenness of the boom made both of us jump, and the nervous shock drove away both the stomach and the head pains.

*   *   *   *   *

Bong! Bong! Bong!

It sounded like an alarm signal. We could hear voices of people rushing about outside, a frightened baby's cry in some other room, and then the triumphant *crowing of a rooster*. Instantly there was a hush among the people in the yard. It lasted for several minutes. Not a sound nor a word could be heard. Then the rooster crowed for a second time. There was no answer from other roosters. A strange thing indeed. I remember noticing the utter absence of the usual barn-yard concert. There was an excited jabbering going on outside, but now it sounded happy—not angry. People were laughing. Perhaps the crowing of the rooster had been a good omen.

Five men walked into our room. They were unarmed, and they held bunches of white feathers in their hands. They handed some of the feathers to Weng and me and motioned us to go with them.

When we stepped into the yard I was surprised to find it deserted. Half a minute before many excited people had been there. It seemed impossible that a crowd could have disappeared so quickly.

The men led us out into the street, and we marched all the way round the quarters, coming at last to a gate where a man stood holding a lantern on a bamboo stick. He demanded a password, and our guide responded with something I could not understand; then the sentry opened a heavy wooden door, which screeched on its hinges. Each man handed the gatekeeper a feather, and both Weng and I mechanically followed their example. The door behind us slammed shut. I heard the key turn in the lock.

*　　*　　*　　*　　*

A faint odour of incense reached us now. In front of me was a table covered with a white cloth upon which were incense burners, and two cups filled with some sort of liquid. The men took off their coats. They stood in front of me half-naked, and one of them instructed Weng and me to stand on the other side of the table and to unbutton our shirts. From a lacquer tray we were handed short daggers by the fifth man. The oldest man lifted the dagger over the incense and murmured a prayer.

I did not like those daggers. For all I knew they might be going to slaughter us.

Then the dagger was placed in front of me, and Weng was told to explain to me that I must hold the dagger over the incense, and swear in my own language to obey the rules of The Hall of Righteous Heroes. I did not even cross my fingers or put my tongue in my cheek, but swore a frightful oath in my most forceful English to obey the rules and regulations of the "benevolent" society whose members sat in The Hall of the Righteous Heroes.

I liked the name—" Righteous Heroes ! "

When I was through somebody tapped a small gong, and each of the Chinese cut himself on the left shoulder with the dagger. Then they wiped away the blood with another of the white feathers, which were then put in a censer and burned. When Weng and I had gone through the same ordeal we were told to put our hands over the bowls, lift the bowls from the table, and turn round.

What was going to happen next ? To turn our backs on five desperate-looking men with daggers in their hands in a darkened room—not so good. However, we obeyed. The five men went round the table and stood in front of us. Weng and I still held the bowls in our hands. After a little while we were led to a door which we had not seen before, and one of our Chinese mentors knocked upon it. They spoke rapidly to Weng, who in turn told me that I was supposed to answer with the word "hou" (Cantonese for "good" or "very well") to everything I was asked. The door opened dramatically, revealing two men standing on the other side of it, but the sudden light blinded me. Somebody asked me something, and following instructions I answered " hou," and then I took two steps forward.

I was in the back courtyard. Men were squatting around on the ground, forming a wide circle. Right in front of me Wong To Ping was sitting, holding another bunch of feathers in his hand. He looked very stern, like a hangman waiting for a condemned criminal to be brought in on the eve of execution.

I stopped just within the gate. Weng stood beside me. The guards came up to us, took feathers from the bunch we carried in our hands, dipped them in the liquid in the bowls, and told us to open our mouths. Then they tickled our throats with the feathers. The result was immediate and inevitable. I almost dropped the bowl, so complete was my surprise.

I heard loud exclamations of "hou! hou!" around me. Whether they were directed at my tormentor or at myself, I do not know. Someone gave me a towel to wipe my mouth and face. Now this was considerate!

A man dressed in some kind of yellow robes came to us, unbuttoned our shirts again, and pointed to the scratches on our shoulders, and addressed loud questions to the audience. Everybody answered "hou! hou!" and then another man brought a single white feather from Wong To Ping and placed it in my hand.

Above us the sky was dark, except for myriads of cold stars. The audience grew silent, and finally Wong To Ping arose. With exaggerated ceremoniousness, he walked up to us and asked something in Chinese, which I, of course, did not understand; but I answered faithfully "hou!" Then he asked the same question of Weng and received the same reply.

The yellow-robed priest went away and returned with a covered basket. It was placed in the middle of the yard. One of the five men who had officiated in the blood ceremony came and handed me the dagger. We were told to uncover the basket, and the moment we did so two roosters that had been imprisoned within them crowed vigorously. Again the exclamation of "hou! hou!" went around the circle.

I think all the other roosters in the village answered our birds. This seemed to be a good omen. Now Wong To Ping approached and ordered us to drink the liquid in the bowls. It was a sticky, salty concoction which threatened to have the same effect as the feather in the throat. Still, I forced the stuff down, and again I heard the exclamation of "hou! hou!" The cup had been covered all the time with a porcelain lid, and when I looked at Weng I could see that he too had difficulty in swallowing the drink. It must have been blood. It had tasted like blood, and I could now see red stains in the bowl. Wong To Ping told us to repeat his words, and as well as I could I did repeat them. Wong To Ping seemed to take himself and the ceremony very seriously.

Then I was told to bend back the head of the rooster and cut its throat. The blood gushed out, and a man leaped forward to catch it in a cup. At the same time Weng slit the neck of his fowl. I knew that if they requested me to drink this blood I would not be able to do it. The whole thing was becoming thoroughly disgusting. Even for the sake of adventure I would have hesitated to go through any more of it. But to my surprise I was told to cut up the rooster. When I had done this Wong To Ping pointed to the heart, and indicated that I should give it to him. He stretched out his hands, and I saw that he wore a strange ring, made of gold and set with a great cornelian engraved with mystic signs. Some of the other men wore the same kind of ring, but I doubt if theirs were gold. I now handed the warm heart of the chicken to Wong To Ping. My hands were messy and red with blood. He took the heart eagerly and ate it. Afterwards he placed another white feather in his mouth, pulled it out red with blood, handed it to me, and indicated by signs that I was to blow it up in the air. It floated down, and the man in yellow robes picked it up. The same ceremony was performed when Weng killed his rooster; then both feathers were burned.

That ended the ceremony. Weng and I were now members of The Hall of Righteous Heroes; in other words, we had become full-fledged bandits.

* * * * *

I slept heavily all night, but in the morning I had a bad taste in my mouth. I watched the sun rise and felt better, and then Wong To Ping sent a man for me.

The old man wanted to know if I would be ready to go to Macao the following morning.

I replied that I would.

Then Wong To Ping said he was going to send several bags of money to be deposited with certain people in Macao. He would give us half of a chit that had been torn in two. The other part should be handed to us by the party who was to receive the money, and if the two parts did not fit the money should not be given away.

I asked how much there was of it. I wanted to know the amount I was to be responsible for.

" Several thousands of dollars," he said.

If I, being a foreigner and a white man, landed in Macao with bags nobody would suspect they contained money belonging to Wong To Ping. I had sworn by the blood of the white rooster to be loyal to the members of The Hall of Righteous Heroes, and he could not but trust that I would bring the money safely to Macao.

He said he would have the money ready the next day. We should sail before daybreak, and he would send two of his men to help me carry the bags. We were to avoid the Cone, a big island with a rocky cone in the middle of it. He had heard that Wong Kiu's men had been seen thereabouts. Then Wong To Ping asked about Weng's foot, because he had noticed that the boy had limped during the initiation ceremony.

When he mentioned the initiation ceremony I ventured to ask him a few questions. Being a Righteous Hero, I wanted to know how many we really were.

"One hundred and forty," he answered. Then he corrected himself, "One hundred and forty-two."

He showed me the great seal of the Hall, a block of soapstone carved in the shape of a dragon.

Then I asked who wore the big rings.

Only the worthy ones, I was told. Men who did valiant deeds beneficial to the Hall. The individual did not exist. Apparently I had been mistaken in believing Wong To Ping only to be the boss of a gang of robbers, who worked for him for a share in the plunder.

"We take from the rich and give to the poor," he announced. That was a beautiful sentiment, surrounded by an aura of Robin Hood philosophy.

"When we kidnap a rich man," he explained, "we hold him for ransom, and when the ransom is paid the sick and poor invariably get the first benefit of the proceeds."

Later he explained some of the secrets of his kidnapping organizations.

Whenever a rich victim is found, even in the far cities of other provinces, and this victim appears to be within reaching distance of Wong To Ping's long-armed

organization, he is kidnapped and brought to the village.
Sometimes it happened that some other pirate chief also
wanted to get hold of the same man, and when this chief
learned that his proposed victim had already been
kidnapped, he often bidded for the purchase of the prisoner.
The fact that there is an actual traffic in kidnapped
victims has given birth to a spy system within the enemy
camps. Whenever a name is mentioned as a prospective
" customer " there is very little doubt that the information
will leak out, and there will be a general rush for possession
of the victim. The first gang to lay hands on him usually
benefits most, and it is to the interest of the victim to
have himself ransomed as soon as possible, before he is
resold, because each sale raises the final figure. If for some
reason the money is not paid the victim is tortured, and
his relatives are informed of the fact ; then if the money
is still not forthcoming he is killed. Strangulation,
decapitation, or stabbing in the heart are the three most
common methods of execution. Shooting, surprisingly
enough, is very seldom used. The other prisoners are
always invited to " look-see " what happens to a man who
is not promptly ransomed.

I asked a blunt question : " How many have you
caused to be killed, Wong To Ping ? "

" Not many," he replied, laughing.

Was it true, I asked him, that he had eaten the livers
or hearts of murdered victims, and that he had drunk the
blood, as he had been accused of doing ?

He answered casually that he did not himself drink
blood and eat human hearts, but he knew that some of
his men did. Then he continued to give me instructions.

As soon as I reached Macao I should have a picture
made for him and bring it back at once. In case I was not

going to return immediately I should give it to the English-speaking servant—not the Russian-speaking one—he cautioned. Why I was not to give it to the latter I never learned.

Then the audience was ended, and I returned to my room.

*   *   *   *   *

There was a change in the behaviour of the other inhabitants of the house and the village. I was looked upon somewhat as a curiosity, but there was no trace of unfriendliness in the gaze of the people. I was one of them now, and I was going on an important mission the next morning. The whole village knew about it. Rumours and news travel fast in China.

I ventured out on the street, accompanied by the limping Weng. Nobody turned us back or asked us where we were going. It was evident that the ceremonies of the night before had brought all this to pass. In the evening the man who had worn the yellow robes came to visit me. He stood in the door and bowed and shook his own hands for an interminable length of time and in a most emphatic manner. I greeted him politely and asked him to what I was indebted for the pleasure of his visit.

Oh, he had brought me my characters and seal, engraved on a little wooden block. I was greatly surprised and grateful. What did my characters mean?

Wong To Ping had called me the "Beneficent Scholar." When he pronounced my name in Chinese to Weng I could not help being startled, because "beneficent scholar" is pronounced almost as my real name. It sounded like Li Lai Assi. It was dangerously near the way my name is pronounced, and I still wonder whether or not Wong To Ping really knew my name

at that time, and if he ever believed that I was a poor
Russsian looking for a job for myself and a few of my
friends. Li Lai Assi sounded too much like Lilius.

*   *   *   *   *

Before daybreak the next morning Weng and I were
out. Wong To Ping wanted to see us. Were we ready to
go ? We should take all our belongings with us.

We marched over the courtyards, and soon we stood
before Wong To Ping, who had been sleeping and was
still in his underwear. I could not but admire his physique.
He was all muscle and sinew. When he moved his
muscles played like those of some superb wild animal.

On the floor beside him were three sacks of money—
three common jute bags.

" How much money is there ?" I asked.

" Never mind," he said, and then handed me one-
half of the chit he had spoken of the day before. The
other half was going to be sent to Macao by a messenger,
and I should keep the money by me wherever I went
until it was demanded by somebody who produced the
other half of the chit. I promised to do so.

But the main thing was to get the photograph, he said,
and here was the camera. He handed it to me, my
beloved kodak, together with all the films.

Both the English-speaking and the Russian-speaking
Chinese appeared in a little while to receive Wong To
Ping's instructions ; then we all marched down the
long, winding path to the river. It took us a whole
hour to get down to the harbour, for the sacks were
cumbersome and heavy. Finally the men decided to
hang them on poles and carry them on their shoulders.
After that we got along a little better.

The *sampan* was waiting for us, and we wiggled ourselves out to the junk, a common fishing-boat, judging from its appearance. As soon as the men saw us coming they ran up the sails, but there was no wind. The current carried us downstream, but it was slow going. There was never a stir of wind, and the blazing sun beat upon us. It was hot, indeed, although it was late fall ; and when we finally came out of the mouth of the river we could see the sea all around us immovable as an immense silvery mirror, with far-off islands appearing to float high up in the air.

A small rowboat passed us scornfully, and I was not surprised at all when the woman who sculled it offered to take us in tow. Our captain and the crew felt that they had "lost face." Then the woman asked a few questions, and the men answered her, and she continued on her way. The English-speaking man scolded the crew for talking to the woman. How did they know she was not a spy. They laughed at him.

With the tide coming in we were almost pushed back to the river, but in the very late afternoon, when the sun had sunk almost to the horizon, there came a faint breeze. I blessed the Gods of the Winds, and so did the crew. Fire-crackers were burned, and incense sticks were stuck in every crevice on board, and then the English-speaking one suggested that we should try to reach the nearest land to stay over-night. When the day darkened I could see a grass hut at a distance on the slope of the lonely hill of the island, and I told Weng to tell the two men that we were going ashore and would take the money with us. I hated to sleep on board with all those murderers around me.

The captain, or Number One man, sniffed the air,

and said that we would have a storm not later than to-morrow. The sunset was flaming scarlet red.

There was another reason why I did not wish to remain on board. I had soon found out that the ship was full of vermin, and although I have lived a long time in China and among the Chinese, I have never become hardened to such things. Some Chinese seem to believe that if the vermin leave you you are out of luck, because the vermin have a way of knowing when a person is going to die.

Taking my five men, I went ashore shortly after dark. I instructed the junk-captain—in my position I was now able to give orders—to remain on board the ship with all his men so as to be ready to sail early the next morning, or at a moment's notice. Under no circumstances was he to leave the bay without me. Having made these things clear to him, I led my five men to the deserted hut, which was located about a quarter of a mile from the shore.

It was the usual grass hut, built on piling. Weng had taken along some rice which we cooked, and then we prepared to sleep. The floor of the house was of bamboo, and very uncomfortable to sleep upon, but all in all it was better than spending the night on board the vermin-infested junk.

This hut consisted of three rooms. Weng and I divided the night into watches. I don't know whether Wong To Ping's servants remained awake or not, but I think that they did not.

Anyway, the night passed peacefully enough. Nothing happened.

But when daylight came things were in a fair way to begin happening very soon.

I had arisen about 6.0 a.m., and the first thing that I saw was our junk scudding out to sea, and four long war-canoes heading into the little harbour. They were fully manned with armed pirates, and they looked as though they meant business.

I wakened my men and pointed to the pirates. They gave one look, and then rushed out of the house and headed for the woods. I've never seen worse cravens than those four Chinese.

By this time the pirates were ashore. As they caught sight of the fleeing guard they opened fire on them with rifles, and in the faint light I could see spurts of white dust jumping up all around them as they ran. I prayed that they would stop some lead, but a rain of bullets began tearing through the flimsy house all around me, cutting short my prayer.

Plucky little Weng had stayed by me when the others ran away. Now he grabbed my arm and motioned towards a hole in the floor. The bullets were jerking splinters off the bamboo rafters all around us, so I did not stop to argue. We dropped through the hole one after the other, and lay flat on the ground.

I always go unarmed; so there was nothing to do but take what cover I could and await developments. Apparently the pirates were taking no chances. They believed that I had not left the building, and they were determined to riddle it thoroughly before coming to collect the loot—which they probably reasoned would be much more easily taken from a dead man's hands than from those of a living man. They had spread out along the rocky hill-side that sloped down to the beach, and were sending a regular hail of bullets through the hut. I could feel splinters and dust falling upon me in a shower.

I was fairly safe for the time being—but God ! how uncomfortable ! I was lying in a nest of fire-ants. If one has never had such an experience with bullets flying about one's ears, one has got something coming. I lay there in abject misery, not daring to move for fear of attracting the enemy's attention. Poor Weng had an indescribable expression upon his face which was laughable even then.

The fire continued without letting up for five or ten minutes. During that time our bamboo hut was absolutely riddled. Then we heard a yell and some shots from the woods. The pirates turned their attention away from us for a moment, and I ventured to raise my head. A dozen or more of Wong To Ping's men were coming out from the trees, darting from rock to rock, shooting as they came. They were a party that the wily old pirate had taken the precaution to send along to keep an eye on us. At the sound of the first shots they had come rushing across the island at the double-quick.

*   *   *   *   *

But my fun was just beginning. Apparently the pirates knew about me and the money-bags, and they were determined to have that money. While the main body of pirates held off the relief party one burly fellow came running toward the house. I saw him coming and climbed back up through the hole in the floor. He came up the bamboo ladder at the same instant, and for a moment we stood facing each other, with the money-bags between us on the floor.

The pirate must have been surprised to see me alive after the bombardment that had been directed at the house, but he was game. Wrenching off one of the

Q

bamboo rungs of the entrance ladder, he came at me.
I heaved the money sacks through the holes in the floor
to Weng, who dragged them off as speedily as the weight
of the bags would permit. The pirate and I tangled.

It was a hot fight while it lasted. He seemed to be
everywhere at once, clouting me with his club, now on
the shoulders, now on the back, now on the ribs. Once
I threw up my arm to shield my face, and caught a
terrific blow on the biceps. That made my left arm use-
less. Then he gave me a rapid blow on the right side,
fracturing two ribs ; his next one caved in a rib on my
left side. I was beginning to totter, when some of Wong
To Ping's men came rushing up to the house, and my
assailant fled. They shot him as he ran and brought him
back bound. I think he died later.

I looked about for Weng, but could not find him
anywhere. I called him, and heard a faint answer not
very far away. The answer came from the bushes, and
I yelled again, expecting to see him emerging from the
underbrush ; but when he did not answer at once I
became uneasy and told one of the men to go down and
see what had happened.

At that instant Weng appeared. He walked slowly
and with difficulty. He was very pale, and large drops
of blood were dripping from his left sleeve.

" Are you shot, Weng ? "

" A little."

I could move only with difficulty, but still I managed
to get his shirt off. The bullet had passed through his
left shoulder. It was rather near the throat, but I hoped
that it might not be as dangerous as it seemed.

" Does it hurt much ? " I asked.

" Not much, but blood come my mouth."

This did not sound very good. By now the others had joined us, and our brave captain had returned to the bay with his junk. I wondered what Wong To Ping would have done with him had he been present. I bound up Weng's wound with strips of my shirt, and two men led him down to the shore, steadying him as he went. The poor boy was pale, and I was getting an honest scare lest his wound should prove more serious than I had made it out to be.

" Do you think you can go down to the boat, or shall we carry you ? "

" Can do ! " he said. " Can do ! " Then he fainted.

We carried him aboard the junk, and spread a straw mat for him to lie upon. We washed his wound with hot water, but he did not regain consciousness. We set sail, and about noontime we saw the hills of Macao looming up to the north-east.

Weng never moved. His breathing was fast and his pulse beat furiously.

He died when the first row of white houses came clearly in sight, and I held his hand until the warmth of life had departed from him.

*   *   *   *   *

They hid him down below. The Macao authorities were not to know that a man had died from a bullet wound while on board a mysterious junk.

I had learned to love this loyal chap, and I felt the blow hard enough to wish that I had never started on my foolhardy adventure. We had become friends, and all the " copy " in the world and all the praise of editors could not pay for the loss of the life of a friend.

And so the latest member of The Hall of Righteous Heroes went to his ancestors.

The money was safely brought to Macao and delivered into the hands of two men who produced the other half of the chit which I carried. Wong To Ping's two men, the Russian-speaking and the English-speaking ones, had disappeared.

I went to the hotel, got a room, and became "myself" again. I liked the beard I had grown, but it was much improved by the ministrations of a barber. But the greatest luxury of all was a hot bath and a general clean-up.

Weng's death rested heavily on my conscience. I felt that I was responsible for his misadventure. If it had not been for me he would probably have stayed home around the rice-pots.

Still, it was no good brooding over the affair. I tried to take my mind away from it. But I knew now that I should never return to Wong To Ping.

After several days in bed, nursing my bruised ribs, I was up again, moving slowly about, and visiting the old *fan-tan* dens, seeing and learning whatever I had missed on previous occasions. My camera was working overtime. And many a night I spent betting on various numbers and combinations—sometimes winning, sometimes losing.

*   *   *   *   *

There was a knock at the door. A Chinese stood smiling and bowing and speaking in pidgin-English. The man said to me: "I want see you alone."

I whispered to my newly-acquired secretary to go out of the room, but to stand behind the door in case I should need him, and turning to the Chinese I bowed in response to his salutations, and asked him to come in.

I pushed the bell-button and told the boy to bring

Wong To Ping's watch (*p.* 205)

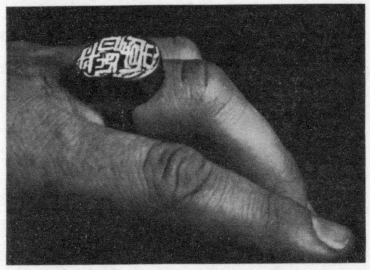

The ring of The Hall of Righteous Heroes

tea. The visitor was a goldsmith, he said, and he had brought me a gift from Wong.

"Which Wong?" I asked, surprised.

Oh, Wong from Lai Chi San. Hadn't I been there recently and become a friend of his?

I looked at him quizzically and did not answer.

With many bows and smiles he handed me a small package.

"Wong vellee vellee pleased. He vellee great man. He thank you vellee, vellee much bring his money here."

I unwrapped the package and opened the little box; in it glimmered a heavy signet ring of virgin gold. It was an exact copy of those which Wong To Ping and some of the other Righteous Heroes of the Hall had worn, except that the characters representing my Chinese name, "Beneficent Scholar," were engraved on it.

Wong To Ping! You are doubtless a murderer, kidnapper, seducer, opium addict, blackmailer, and you may be bound for hell, but I believe that you are a grateful cuss and a gentleman!

The ring is one of my most valued possessions.

CAMBODIA

GEORGE COEDÈS
Angkor

MALCOLM MacDONALD
Angkor and the Khmers*

CENTRAL ASIA

PETER FLEMING
Bayonets to Lhasa

ANDRÉ GUIBAUT
Tibetan Venture

LADY MACARTNEY
An English Lady in
Chinese Turkestan

DIANA SHIPTON
The Antique Land

C. P. SKRINE AND
PAMELA NIGHTINGALE
Macartney at Kashgar*

ERIC TEICHMAN
Journey to Turkistan

ALBERT VON LE COQ
Buried Treasures of
Chinese Turkestan

AITCHEN K. WU
Turkistan Tumult

CHINA

All About Shanghai:
A Standard Guide

L.C. ARLINGTON AND
WILLIAM LEWISOHN
In Search of Old Peking

VICKI BAUM
Shanghai '37

ERNEST BRAMAH
Kai Lung's Golden Hours*

ERNEST BRAMAH
The Wallet of Kai Lung*

ANN BRIDGE
The Ginger Griffin

NIGEL CAMERON
The Chinese Smile

CHANG HSIN-HAI
The Fabulous Concubine*

CARL CROW
Handbook for China

PETER FLEMING
The Siege at Peking

ROBERT FORD
Captured in Tibet

MARY HOOKER
Behind the Scenes in
Peking

NEALE HUNTER
Shanghai Journal*

GEORGE N. KATES
The Years that Were Fat

CORRINNE LAMB
The Chinese Festive
Board

G. E. MORRISON
An Australian in China

DESMOND NEILL
Elegant Flower

PETER QUENNELL
A Superficial Journey
through Tokyo and
Peking

OSBERT SITWELL
Escape with Me! An
Oriental Sketch-book

J. A. TURNER
Kwang Tung or Five Years
in South China

JULES VERNE
The Tribulations of a
Chinese Gentleman

HONG KONG AND MACAU

AUSTIN COATES
City of Broken Promises

AUSTIN COATES
A Macao Narrative

AUSTIN COATES
Macao and the British

AUSTIN COATES
Myself a Mandarin

AUSTIN COATES
The Road

The Hong Kong Guide
1893

INDONESIA

DAVID ATTENBOROUGH
Zoo Quest for a Dragon*

VICKI BAUM
A Tale from Bali*

'BENGAL CIVILIAN'
Rambles in Java and the
Straits in 1852

MIGUEL COVARRUBIAS
Island of Bali*

AUGUSTA DE WIT
Java: Facts and Fancies

JACQUES DUMARÇAY
Borobudur

JACQUES DUMARÇAY
The Temples of Java

ANNA FORBES
Unbeaten Tracks in Islands
of the Far East

GEOFFREY GORER
Bali and Angkor

JENNIFER LINDSAY
Javanese Gamelan

EDWIN M. LOEB
Sumatra: Its History and
People

MOCHTAR LUBIS
The Outlaw and Other
Stories

MOCHTAR LUBIS
Twilight in Djakarta

MADELON H. LULOFS
Coolie*

MADELON H. LULOFS
Rubber

COLIN McPHEE
A House in Bali*

ERIC MJÖBERG
Forest Life and Adventures
in the Malay Archipelago

H. W. PONDER
Java Pageant

HICKMAN POWELL
The Last Paradise

F. M. SCHNITGER
Forgotten Kingdoms in
Sumatra

E. R. SCIDMORE
Java, The Garden of the
East

MICHAEL SMITHIES
Yogyakarta: Cultural Heart
of Indonesia

LADISLAO SZÉKELY
Tropic Fever: The
Adventures of a Planter
in Sumatra

EDWARD C. VAN NESS AND
SHITA PRAWIROHARDJO
Javanese Wayang Kulit

HARRY WILCOX
Six Moons in Sulawesi

JAPAN

WILLIAM PLOMER
Sado

MALAYSIA

ODOARDO BECCARI
Wanderings in the Great
Forests of Borneo

ISABELLA L. BIRD
The Golden Chersonese:
Travels in Malaya in
1879

MARGARET BROOKE
THE RANEE OF SARAWAK
My Life in Sarawak

SIR HUGH CLIFFORD
Saleh: A Prince of Malaya

HENRI FAUCONNIER
The Soul of Malaya

W. R. GEDDES
Nine Dayak Nights

C. W. HARRISON
Illustrated Guide to the
Federated Malay States
(1923)

BARBARA HARRISSON
Orang-Utan

TOM HARRISSON
Borneo Jungle

TOM HARRISSON
World Within: A Borneo
Story

CHARLES HOSE
Natural Man

W. SOMERSET MAUGHAM
Ah King and Other Stories*

W. SOMERSET MAUGHAM
The Casuarina Tree*

MARY McMINNIES
The Flying Fox*

ROBERT PAYNE
The White Rajahs of
Sarawak

CARVETH WELLS
Six Years in the Malay
Jungle

SINGAPORE

RUSSELL GRENFELL
Main Fleet to Singapore

R. W. E. HARPER AND
HARRY MILLER
Singapore Mutiny

MASANOBU TSUJI
Singapore 1941–1942

G. M. REITH
Handbook to Singapore
(1907)

C. E. WURTZBURG
Raffles of the Eastern Isles

THAILAND

CARL BOCK
Temples and Elephants

REGINALD CAMPBELL
Teak-Wallah

ANNA LEONOWENS
The English Governess at
the Siamese Court

MALCOLM SMITH
A Physician at the Court
of Siam

ERNEST YOUNG
The Kingdom of the
Yellow Robe

Titles marked with an asterisk have restricted rights.